P9-DTF-621

THE JOY OF
Pastry

DAVID MUNN

BARRON'S

Woodbury, New York • London • Toronto • Sydney

TO MY WIFE, JOAN

ACKNOWLEDGMENTS

Very special thanks to John Lowy and Bill Liederman at the New York Cooking Center for their patience and understanding through the years. Also thanks to the following for teaching and helping me write this book: Lewis Basner, Richard Glavin, Gerald J. Gliber, Arlene Battifarano, Rocky Richardson, Nicholas Malgieri, Albert Kumin, and in fond memory of Florence Hyde.

All inquiries should be addressed to:
Barron's Educational Series, Inc.
113 Crossways Park Drive
Woodbury, New York 11797

Library of Congress Catalog Card No. 85-18665

International Standard Book No. 0-8120-5670-1

Library of Congress Cataloging-in-Publication Data
Munn, David.
 The joy of pastry.
 Includes index.
 1. Pastry. I. Title.
TX773.M86 1985   641.8′65   85-18665
ISBN 0-8120-5670-1

PRINTED IN THE UNITED STATES OF AMERICA

5 6 7 8   9 8 7 6 5 4 3 2 1

Credits
Color photographs: Matthew Klein
Food styling: Andrea Swenson
Photo styling: Linda Cheverton
Props used are courtesy of the following: china from Haviland, silver by Buccellati, and flowers by Very Special Flowers, all of New York City.

Recipe on page 56, reprinted from *Grand Finales* by Dick Teuber;

Recipe on page 194, reprinted from *The Best of Southern Italian Cooking* by J.C. Grasso, both published by Barron's Educational Series, Inc.

CONTENTS

INTRODUCTION

Eating pastry is certainly a joy, although few people would agree on exactly what they consider pastry, let alone on which ones were the best. We could be very strict in our interpretation, and say that pastries are baked foods that are made with a paste of basically flour, butter, and water. But what of meringues, which are just egg whites beaten with sugar? Surely Meringue Petits Fours—crisp ovals sandwiched with pastry cream filling—are pastries to most people. Some pastry "pastes" contain sugar, yet there are countless dishes that use a savory pastry, such as a quiche or a *vol-au-vent* filled to overflowing with sweetbreads and cream sauce. Strictly speaking, a listing of pastries might not include cakes, since they are made with batters, not doughs. Yet when I ask my friends to name their favorite pastries, they omit apple pie (which has a pastry dough crust), and instead list Sacher Torte and Almond Dacquoise.

I feel it best not to attempt any definitions, or even to apply any "textbook" rules to this collection of recipes. For most people, pastry is the fanciful, the elaborate, the delicious, the unusual, the excessive. It is the cake that makes special the conclusion of a dinner meal, but it is also the breakfast brioche, so rich and eggy that it's the perfect beginning for a busy day. It is a flaky strip of puff pastry lined with pastry cream and filled with glazed strawberries, but it is also an afternoon Eclair, a Sunday morning Croissant, a late-night Almond Bear Claw. Pastries can be Danish, French, Italian, Viennese, Middle Eastern. They can be filled or plain, with fruit or a type of cream or custard. They can have nuts, candied fruit, spices, chocolate. Some are yeast-risen, others depend on beaten eggs or egg whites to send them skyward.

Some people like their pastries simple, like a Kugelhopf or a Cheese Danish. Others want them packed with fruit or lightened with cream. Cakes in particular can be layered with mousse, fruit, cream, or jelly; and they can be glazed, iced, frosted, or simply dusted with confectioners sugar. Pies and tarts, puff pastries, cream puffs, Danishes, and layered cakes are to be sampled here. All the pastries in this book are sweet; beyond that, they are simply joyful desserts.

Many of these pastries will be the favorites you immediately think of when you hear the waiter in a restaurant ask, "Would you like something from our pastry cart?" The cart in this case contains some classics like a Paris-Brest, a Linzer Tart, and Napoleons. But take a look on the second shelf, behind the Cream Horns. You'll spy a Strawberry Custard Tart, a Caramelized Pear Tart, a Three-Nut Chocolate Tart, a Cinnamon-Nut Brioche Loaf, an Orange Mocha Cake, and a Strawberry Vacherin. Not far from them are some Phyllo Almond Fingers, White Chocolate Mousse served in Tulip Cups, and an Italian Trifle. You'll even find some non-pastry items on the lower shelf, included here because they are personal favorites as well as popular treats: Fudge Brownies, Hamentashen, Raised Honey Doughnuts, Italian Sweet Ravioli, Lemon Scones, and Crepes with an Apple-Calvados Filling.

Perhaps the greatest joy of all, when it comes to pastry, is making them yourself. Eating pastry is fun, but making it is positively exhilarating. Baking has its challenges and makes its demands of the cook, but the rewards are unmatched. If you make your own pastries, as well as eat them, you'll have the extra joy of creativity—of mixing and matching the components of your pastry and developing your favorite combinations. The Joy of Pastry is a double-joy!

BAKING THE BEST PASTRIES

What is baking and why is it so different from cooking? I often use this question to start off my baking classes because there is no simple answer.

I've heard people say that cooking is an art, while baking is a science. This is certainly an over-simplification, but there is some truth in the statement. All the basic doughs used in baking are leavened in one way or another. It is this leavening process that makes baking more scientific than cooking. Once the basic doughs have been mixed, the "die is cast." If a bread dough, a pie crust, or a cake batter is measured and mixed properly, it should also then rise properly. If it rises properly, the rest is easy.

A cook can adjust the flavor of his or her soup or sauce while on its way to the table, but what can a pastry chef do to a slice of pie or a bun? An incorrect (or unscientific) measurement or procedure early on can easily damage or even prevent essential leavening. Once this happens, there is nothing to be done, no matter how creative or artistic the baker is. The baker can be temperamental or creative only after the initial measurements and mixings have yielded a well-leavened dough or batter.

This is why a basic understanding of baking processes and procedures is so important. Follow all directions closely, and measure all ingredients carefully. Develop a respect for the "science" of baking, and remember that patience and repetition are important in the bakery (as in the laboratory). Don't give up; try it again.

BASIC INGREDIENTS

Most of the ingredients of baking are common items, easily found in supermarkets and familiar to even the most inexperienced of cooks. There are some important things a pastry baker should know, however, before starting.

WHITE FLOUR White flour is steel milled, as opposed to stone ground. It can be mass produced consistently and quickly. Hot steel blades break down the flour, eliminating almost all of its original nutritional value (vitamins, fiber, wheat germ oil, etc.) but leaves intact the essential protein (gluten). Gluten is present in wheat and gives it the elasticity so crucial in baking. White flour is "enriched" because it would otherwise be almost worthless nutritionally. It is also usually bleached and bromated for ease of handling and longer shelf life. I suggest you use unbleached flour in these recipes for best results. All flour measures are for presifted flour taken directly from the package, since almost all flours nowadays are presifted.

WHOLE-WHEAT FLOUR Whole-wheat flour is stone ground, which is a slower and more cumbersome process but which results in a more nutritionally complete flour. Whole-wheat flour contains dozens of vitamins and minerals, not just the four or five re-introduced into enriched white flour. It also is rich in fiber and wheat germ oil, which make it less commercially viable with a shorter shelf life. Fiber and oil also render the flour less glutinous. This means the whole-wheat flour is more healthful than white flour, but less desirable for good structure in a baked good. Combining the flours often yields a happy medium.

SUGAR   Sugar is desirable in baking for its flavor and also for its color when it caramelizes and browns in the heat of the oven. Sugar is available in a variety of forms (brown, confectioners, granulated, superfine) but generally speaking it contains very little nutrition and should not be consumed excessively. The recipes in this book have the minimum amount of sugar in them, and since sugar is often an essential ingredient, I recommend that you follow the measurements closely.

HONEY   Try to use uncooked, unfiltered honey when a recipe calls for it. Honey is cooked to homogenize it and keep it clear and smooth on store shelves. Much of its nutritional value, however, is lost in the cooking process. Bringing it to a temperature above 105°F. will break down the honey's nutritional components. Uncooked honey tends to separate and crystallize on the store shelf, giving it an uneven appearance. It is not only more healthful, but can be made homogeneous and even-textured by placing it briefly in a pot of warm water and stirring from the bottom up.

EGGS Always use large eggs in these recipes. When separating eggs, be careful not to let any part of the yolk get into the whites. To beat whites to highest volume, be certain your beaters and bowl are also spotlessly clean. Room-temperature egg whites usually beat to a higher volume than cold ones.

BUTTER Always use the freshest grade AA sweet butter. All recipes in this book have been planned to be made with sweet butter. Sweet butter does not contain sugar, but is merely salt free. Remember that salt is a preservative and can also hide "off" flavors. Buy unsalted butter and you will be assured the tastiest and freshest results.

CHOCOLATE I prefer semisweet or bittersweet chocolate, and use it in these recipes. When buying chocolate, check the ingredients list to be certain that no artificial ingredients have been used. An inferior chocolate not only tastes inferior but can ruin the texture of your dessert.

CREAM When cream is called for, it is usually heavy cream, which is also known as whipping cream. Buy fresh cream, and avoid the ultrapasteurized variety, since this does not beat up as well and also lacks flavor. To beat cream to highest volume, use chilled beaters and chilled bowl, and chill cream before beating.

LEAVENERS If possible, use cake yeast; it is less processed than dry yeast and is also faster acting. Yeast is the only organic leavener, and it is unique in that it is "alive." Baking soda and baking powder are chemical leaveners and are not alive; this means that they release gas bubbles only once or twice to leaven batter. They lend no flavor or "fermentation" to a baked good.

SALT   Not only a flavoring agent but also an essential yeast inhibitor, salt allows the living yeast to work properly. Too much salt in a yeast-risen dough will prevent the dough from rising, while too little (or none at all) will cause it to over-ferment.

BASIC EQUIPMENT

Depending on the pastries you want to make, you'll need a variety of items, most of which are readily available in supermarkets and cookware shops. Buy good equipment; don't scrimp or you'll only have to replace it when it warps or breaks or—worse yet—ruins your pastries. The following is a list of items that most cooks will need for making pastry.

1. MIXING BOWLS   a variety of sizes, preferably stainless-steel and ceramic.

2. WOODEN SPOONS   with different length handles.

3. RUBBER SPATULAS   3 or 4, of varying widths.

4. WIRE WHISKS   a good assortment, including a couple of balloon whisks, other wire whisks.

5. BAKING PANS   for cakes, you'll need some 8- and 9-inch round pans plus a 10-inch tube pan and a 10-inch Bundt pan.

You'll also need 8- and 9-inch pie pans and some tart pans with removable bottoms.

6. **PASTRY SCRAPER** you'll need this rigid plastic rounded-off square or rectangle to scrape clean the counter and scoop up a dough you are kneading.

7. **SET OF PASTRY BAGS AND TIPS** get a good assortment of tips, including some star and plain tips, as well as several bags of varying sizes.

8. **ROLLING PIN** select a top-quality rolling pin, preferably a ball-bearing type with handles; the rolling pin should be at least 12 inches long.

9. **SIFTER/STRAINER** a flour sifter, plus several strainers to sift flour and strain liquids.

10. **PASTRY BRUSHES** get a couple, with varying widths, made of pure bristle.

11. **FROSTING SPATULA** use a firm, metal spatula with a long blade to spread the frosting over your cake. If possible, also get a drop blade spatula.

12. **ELECTRIC MIXER** although not essential, an electric mixer with strong motor can be useful in beating egg whites and whipping cream.

CREAM PUFF PASTRIES

Cream puff batter is the ideal vehicle for just about any kind of filling, sweet or savory. Being such a simple preparation of eggs, flour, liquid, and butter, it is not meant to be eaten on its own but, rather, filled with rich pastry creams and/or fresh fruits.

Cream puff batter is leavened simply by beaten eggs and the steam that is released by the butter in the mixture when the dough is baked. It can almost double in size during baking, and it is just this dramatic "puffing" that makes it so exciting to bake. A well-prepared cream puff should be light and airy, with a golden brown crust all around. Inside, it will be mostly air and a bit of moist batter.

Don't be frightened when your batter seems different from previous times, even though you seemed to prepare it the same way. Remember that a little more water will evaporate during the boiling stage. Also, eggs and flour always vary a bit in size and texture, so you'll have increasing success each time you work with the batter and become more familiar with its nature.

Eggs are the one ingredient that may be considered a "variable." They are the last ingredient added, and, as such, will determine the texture of the batter. Always add the eggs slowly (one at a time), beating well after each one. Stop adding eggs when the batter begins to "fall away," meaning that it should be just loose enough to shift a bit when you stop mixing but not so loose as to lose its shape on the baking pan. Conversely, a batter that is too stiff will not fully blossom in the oven.

The basic recipe can easily be doubled or tripled (or increased to any size at all) but you will need fewer and fewer eggs each time it is multiplied. For example, a quadruple batch of batter will probably need only twelve or thirteen eggs instead of sixteen, which would be the strict numerical multiplication. If you cannot find large eggs or are not sure how many you've added already, simply stop adding eggs when you've reached the consistency of sour cream. Practicing once or twice will make even the very beginning home-baker confident. Cream puff batter is most forgiving, and those odd-looking shapes will puff up beautifully during the baking process.

The proportions for the basic batter are classic, allowing but little room for variation. Milk may be substituted for all or part of the liquid, but this will make the insides of your puffs moister and more difficult to bake through. Beginners are better off using little or no milk. You'll achieve professional results with a minimum of effort and have a rewarding and pleasurable baking experience in the process. Guests will be amazed at your results and their compliments will inspire you to perhaps try some more difficult recipes.

Practice making cream puffs on a rainy day. You will improve your pastry-bag skills and the results of your efforts can be frozen quite successfully. Frozen puffs can go from freezer directly to the oven and baked for about seven minutes, or until the crusts return. Then let them cool, fill as desired, and decorate as preferred. Drop-in guests will be impressed, and your family will be pleased to have fresh, delicious cream puffs at seemingly a moment's notice.

NOTE: If you grate ½ cup of cheese (Parmesan or Romano work best) into the batter, you'll make crispy, delicious cheese puffs. Or hollow out a split cream puff, place a scoop of ice cream inside, and replace the top, to make a simple and exciting summertime variation.

This batter may be stored (well wrapped) in the refrigerator for several days before use, although fresh batter is always a bit better. It can also be frozen. Thaw overnight in the refrigerator, then use as desired.

Leftover batter can be saved to add to a future batch or mixed with grated cheese to make cheese puffs.

Opposite: Cream Puffs (page 7).
Page following: Eclairs (page 9).

CREAM PUFF BATTER

MAKES 3 TO 4 CUPS

INGREDIENTS

1 cup water
½ cup (1 stick) butter
Pinch of salt
1 cup all-purpose flour
4 large eggs

Cream puff batter—*pâte à chou*—is one of the simplest and most versatile preparations. Fast and easy, this dough can be used in spur-of-the-moment situations for either desserts or appetizers. Everyone always has a little flour, butter, and some eggs. Add some cream or milk, chocolate or preserves, and you've got eclairs. No equipment at all is necessary, except for an oven.

1 Put water, butter, and salt in a heavy-gauge pot set over medium heat and bring to a boil. Make sure that all the butter melts into the liquid before the water comes to a boil. As soon as the liquid boils, add the flour at once, stir well, and remove the pot momentarily from the heat.

2 Continue beating the mixture with a paddle or wooden spoon for a few minutes or until most of the steam has dissipated. When the mixture has cooled somewhat, add the first egg, beating it into the batter as you add it. It is important that the mixture isn't too hot when you add the egg, because adding it prematurely can cause it to scramble. Add each subsequent egg

Opposite: Fresh Fruit Baskets (page 13).
Page preceding: Paris-Brest (page 11).

after the previous one has been absorbed into the mixture. As you add the last egg and mix it in, the mixture should begin to fall away from the paddle or wooden spoon.

3 Keep mixing the batter for several minutes to smooth it out and lighten it. By stirring the mixture well, you trap air bubbles and promote a lighter and puffier result. The batter should now be thin enough to flow smoothly through a pastry tip, but not so thin as to spread out and lose definition on the baking sheet.

4 Pipe out the batter as desired, depending on whether you are making cream puffs, eclairs, or another pastry. Follow directions for individual pastries to bake at appropriate temperature and for desired length.

NOTE Four eggs are always needed for making a small quantity of batter, as in this recipe. However, when this recipe is multiplied for a larger quantity, use proportionately fewer. For instance, if making a triple batch, use 10 or 11 eggs, not 12.

CREAM PUFFS

INGREDIENTS

1 batch Cream Puff Batter
1 cup heavy cream
1 teaspoon granulated
  sugar
1 teaspoon vanilla extract

PASTRY CREAM

2 cups milk
¾ cup granulated sugar
6 large egg yolks
Pinch of salt
1½ teaspoons vanilla
  extract
⅓ cup all-purpose flour
2 tablespoons butter

1 Preheat the oven to 350°F. Lightly grease a large baking sheet. Place the batter in a large pastry bag fitted with a no. 4 or no. 5 star tip. Pipe out *fleurettes* about the size of a Ping-Pong ball—not too large—and about 4 inches apart. They should "puff" quite a bit in the oven.

2 Bake puffs for about 25 minutes, or until the puffs are lightly browned all over and crispy. Remove from baking sheet to a rack and let cool.

3 Meanwhile, prepare the pastry cream. Heat the milk with half the sugar in a heavy stainless-steel or enamel pot. (Don't use aluminum because it will react with the ingredients and cause a greenish tinge.) Whisk the sugar with the milk until it dissolves. Keep warm. Beat together the yolks and remaining sugar in a large mixing bowl, then add the salt and vanilla, and mix until smooth. Add the flour slowly, whisking it into the yolk mixture.

4 Bring the milk to a rolling boil, then whisk about ⅓ of it into the yolk mixture to temper it. Bring the remaining ⅔s of the milk mixture back to a rolling boil over medium heat and whisk in the tempered yolk mixture. Don't stop whisking the custard as it thickens, lest it start to lump up.

5 Place the butter in the bottom of a cool mixing bowl and have it ready for the custard. When the custard begins to boil and the flour in it is cooked (you will notice a perking on the surface), immediately pour the custard through a sieve onto the butter in the bowl. Whisk the butter into the custard until it melts, then cover the custard with plastic wrap, pressing the plastic lightly onto the surface of the custard. Chill briefly.

6 Whip the heavy cream with the teaspoon of sugar and flavor it with the vanilla. Fold the whipped cream into the pastry cream and keep it cool until ready to fill the puffs.

7 When the puffs have cooled, fit a pastry bag with a no. 2 plain tip and fill the bag with pastry cream. Pipe the filling into each of the puffs, injecting it through the bottoms. Alternatively, you could cut the puffs in half, fill them with the cream, and then replace the tops.

NOTE The filling and puffs can both be made ahead, but once assembled, the cream puffs are best eaten the same day.

ECLAIRS

Photo 2 following page 4

MAKES ABOUT 1 DOZEN

INGREDIENTS

1 batch Cream Puff Batter

1 batch Pastry Cream (see previous recipe)

1 cup heavy cream

1 teaspoon granulated sugar

1 teaspoon vanilla extract

CHOCOLATE GLAZE

8 ounces semisweet chocolate, chopped

1/2 cup heavy cream

2 teaspoons vanilla extract

2 tablespoons butter

Classic and beautiful, these eclairs may be piped large or small, but remember that they must be filled and glazed—and very thin or flat shapes make the filling difficult.

1 Preheat the oven to 350°F. Lightly grease a large baking sheet.

2 Place the batter in a large pastry bag fitted with a no. 4 or no. 5 star tip. Pipe out fingers of batter onto the baking sheet about 3 inches apart. The fingers can be made rippled or plain by moving the nozzle straight or wavering it. Squeeze steadily for even fingers.

3 Bake fingers for about 25 minutes, or until they are lightly browned all over and crispy. Remove from baking sheet to a rack and let cool.

4 Meanwhile, prepare the filling, following steps 4 through 6 in the Cream Puff recipe. Whip the cream with the teaspoon of sugar and flavor with vanilla, then mix with the cooled pastry cream.

5 Also have the chocolate glaze ready. In the top of a double boiler, melt the chocolate with the cream, vanilla, and butter until smooth. Keep warm.

6 Eclairs are prettiest and most fun to eat when the filling is piped in from either end. Fit a pastry bag with a no. 2 plain tip and fill bag with the lightened pastry cream. Pipe the filling into the eclairs, making sure that it goes all the way through to the other side.

7 Hold the eclair in your hand and dip the entire top into the chocolate glaze. Set on a rack to harden the glaze and then serve.

NOTE Once again as with cream puffs, the components may be prepared in advance and assembled just before serving. Otherwise, keep them refrigerated. These are best served the same day as made.

PARIS-BREST

Photo 3 following page 4

SERVES 8 TO 10

INGREDIENTS

1 batch Cream Puff Batter
1 egg, lightly beaten
½ cup slivered almonds
1 pint fresh strawberries,
  washed and hulled
¼ cup fruit-flavored
  liqueur (optional)
2 cups heavy cream
1 tablespoon granulated
  sugar
1 teaspoon vanilla extract
Confectioners sugar

1 Preheat the oven to 350°F. Lightly grease a large baking sheet.

2 Place the batter in a large pastry bag fitted with a no. 5 star tip. Pipe out a 12-inch oval onto the baking sheet, then pipe out a 10-inch oval inside the larger one. Now pipe out a series of *fleurettes* (or shells) around the oval above and in between the 2 ovals. If there are any sharp points or edges on the *fleurettes,* use a pastry brush to gently press them smooth. Glaze the ring with the beaten egg, using a soft pastry brush, to give the batter a nice shine and color when it bakes. Sprinkle the oval with the slivered almonds.

3 Bake the cream puff ring longer than you would think necessary, especially for a cake as large as this. Allow at least 30 minutes, or until the crust is firm and dark. The nuts will also toast until very dark, but do not let them burn. Cream puff pastries release steam after baking, and this steam subsequently softens the crust and sometimes causes it to flatten or even collapse. By baking the oval a little longer, there is less chance it will collapse. When done, remove from baking sheet and let cool on a rack.

4 While the oval is cooling, prepare the strawberries. Slice each from stem to tip into thin slices. If desired, macerate them for a short while in a liqueur.

5 Prepare the filling. Whip the cream until it forms soft peaks, then sprinkle in the sugar and vanilla and continue to whip until it forms stiff peaks.

6 At least 30 minutes after the oval has come out of the oven, slice it in half horizontally, using a sharp serrated knife, so as not to damage the delicate crust. Remove the top carefully and set aside.

7 Place the flavored whipped cream in a pastry bag fitted with a no. 6 star tip and pipe out onto the bottom half of the oval all the way around. Distribute the strawberries on top of the cream, placing them to the outside of the ring. You want the strawberry tips to show through the layers, sticking out in a nice arrangement around the outer edge.

8 Sprinkle confectioners sugar on the top of the oval and place it gently over the strawberries. Serve at once.

FRESH FRUIT BASKETS

Photo opposite page 5

MAKES ABOUT 1 DOZEN

INGREDIENTS

1 batch Cream Puff Batter

½ batch Pastry Cream (see Cream Puff recipe)

1 cup heavy cream

1 teaspoon granulated sugar

1 teaspoon vanilla extract

2 cups sliced fresh fruits in season, such as strawberries, raspberries, peaches, kiwifruit

1 cup pure raspberry preserves

1 tablespoon fruit liqueur, such as framboise or Grand Marnier

These are a perfect summer pastry. Any fruits in season can be combined for delicious and colorful variations.

1 Preheat the oven to 350°F. Lightly grease a large baking sheet.

2 Place the batter in a large pastry bag fitted with a no. 4 or 5 star tip. Pipe out larger circles than for cream puffs, about 2½ inches in diameter. Leave from 2 to 3 inches between them to allow for even baking and adequate puffing.

3 Bake puffs for about 20 minutes, or until the puffs are well browned and lightly crusted. Remove from baking sheet to a rack and let cool completely.

4 Meanwhile, prepare the filling. Make the pastry cream as described in steps 3 through 5 on page 7. Then whip the heavy cream with the sugar and flavor with vanilla. Fold in the pastry cream and keep cool until ready to use.

5 When puffs are completely cool, slice off the tops about ¼ of the way down. Remove any wet dough from the insides of the puffs with a small spoon and discard. Place about 1 tablespoon of the lightened pastry cream in each bottom and then arrange several small pieces of sliced fruit on top and coming slightly over the edge.

6 Bring the raspberry preserves to a boil in a small saucepan and then strain to remove large pieces or seeds. Whisk in the liqueur. Glaze each top liberally with the preserve glaze. Replace the lids but allow the fruit to peek through between the lid and the basket. Drip the remaining glaze over the fruit baskets, allowing the glaze to cascade down the sides. Serve at room temperature immediately, or chill to serve later the same day.

PIES AND TARTS

There are basically two kinds of pie crust: one is flaky, while the other is crumbly. Flaky pie crust (*pâte brisée*) contains little or no sugar and is prepared quickly by rubbing the fat and dry ingredients together, leaving a very coarse texture, and then by adding liquid (egg and/or water or milk) to bind and to allow you to handle the dough. Flaky pie crust is the dough used to make pies, as opposed to tarts. Pies are generally baked in a round, slope-sided pan. Often, also, pies are baked with a top crust.

Tart crust (*pâte sucrée*) does contain sugar and can be prepared in the same manner as flaky crust. However, the more the fat is rubbed into the flour, the less flaky the resulting crust will be. If you rub it very fine and distribute the fat very evenly through the flour, you'll end up with a cookie-type crust. Also, if you prefer a sweeter taste, cream together the fat and the sugar before mixing it briefly with the flour. On hot days the added sugar can result in a very sticky dough, which is hard to handle. Try to work quickly when it is warm and then chill the dough for one full hour before using.

Tarts are usually open faced (without a top crust), and baked in a straight-sided, shallow pan with a crimped edge.

Sticking to hard-and-fast rules in baking would, of course, serve no purpose—whether in a commercial bakery or at home. Combining the various crusts, fillings, and molds is not dangerous, and it even may result in an original which is just perfect for you. For example, my Strawberry Custard Tart has a flaky crust that is only slightly sweet.

Fat and flour are the two basic components in any pie crust (usually three parts flour, two parts fat, one part liquid). A liquid (milk, egg, water) is necessary only to the degree to which it binds the dough and makes it possible for you to roll it out and shape it. Fat shortens the distance a strand of gluten can be stretched; this is why all fats are called shortenings. A "short" dough, such as the pie crust recipes in this book, is handled very little because it contains a high proportion of fat. All of this results in flakiness and tenderness when the fat steams in the oven and melts into the dough.

Vegetable shortening, margarine, and lard have higher melting points than butter. Butter melts at 85°F., about fourteen degrees less than normal body temperature. This means that butter pastries literally melt in your mouth, while others may leave a greasy residue behind. This residue left on the roof of your mouth indicates the baker's desire to substitute cheaper shortenings for butter. The surest indication of butter is its distinctive and delicious flavor.

Many old favorite pie crust recipes include a tablespoon or two of lard or shortening. This enabled bakers in the past (before good refrigeration) to handle their doughs without ruining them. Also, the higher melting point of the shortening allowed for more flaking and tenderness. Many people still prefer a combination of the two.

Whole-wheat flour works beautifully in pie and tart crusts. A pie crust made with about 50 percent whole-wheat flour will have a delicious nutty flavor and a dark brown color. Remember that whole-wheat flour is laden with bran and oil, factors bound to affect the structure of your crust. But most of all, too much coarse flour can overwhelm your crust. If you want to incorporate more whole grains into your diet, gradually increase the amount of whole-wheat flour in your recipe to give the uninitiated a chance to develop a taste for it.

PREBAKING THE PASTRY SHELL   Pie crusts are often baked first and then filled. To prebake a shell, line the pie crust with greased aluminum foil and fill with beans, rice, or baking weights. Be sure to pack the foil along the walls of the shell and in the crease between the sides and the bottom. This is to ensure that the crust flakes up but does not distort too badly, or even collapse at the sides.

Bake the crust with the foil and beans in a 350°F. oven for about 10 to 15 minutes, or until the very edge of the shell just begins to brown. Remove the foil and beans, save the beans for another time you'll be prebaking a shell, and return the crust to the oven for about 10 to 15 minutes more, or until the center of the crust is just golden brown. Prebaked shells can be easily frozen.

Prebaked shells are used with some fruit tarts in which the fruit—especially strawberries, raspberries, and kiwifruit—is best when fresh and unbaked, whereas fruits such as apples and pears stand up to extended heat and can be baked together with a bottom—and perhaps a top—crust or lattice-work.

FLAKY PIE CRUST

MAKES ENOUGH FOR TWO 9-INCH CRUSTS

INGREDIENTS

2 cups all-purpose flour
1½ tablespoons granulated
  sugar
½ teaspoon salt
10 tablespoons butter
1 large egg
2 tablespoons ice water

This recipe makes a flaky, slightly sweet crust that can be used in a number of pies and tarts.

1 Mix together the flour, sugar, and salt in a large bowl. Cut the butter into small pieces and begin working it into the flour with your fingertips, cutting it in very quickly. Butter knives and pastry cutters are cooler to work with, but I prefer my fingertips because of their ability to feel the dough.

2 Toss and work the flour and fat until each piece of butter is about the size of a raisin. Do this quickly, and you will have no trouble with the butter warming.

3 Mix together the egg and water in a small bowl, then add that to the flour and fat mixture. Smear this mixture and knead through it once or twice with the heel of your hand until it barely holds together. Over-working this dough will cause it to become tough; a coarse, marblized texture is what is desired. Immediately flatten the dough into a disc shape, wrap it in clear plastic, and chill in refrigerator for at least 30 minutes. After chilling, the dough is ready to be rolled out and used in recipes.

ROLLING OUT THE DOUGH When you are ready, roll out the chilled dough on a lightly floured surface. If the crust is very cold and begins to crack, you may pound it gently with a rolling pin until the butter softens up slightly. Scrape up the crust and rotate it often while rolling, being certain that the work surface is always lightly floured. Toss the flour across the surface to spread it evenly.

If the dough does not move beneath the rolling pin, it will be stuck to the table. Do not let this happen, or the dough will not flake properly. Because of the delicate nature of its structure, the dough cannot be reworked. If you are careful in chilling, rolling, rotating, and dusting the dough, it will be easy to handle and you will have a tender and flaky crust.

When the dough is rolled to a thickness of about ⅛ inch, place it in the desired pie or tart pan and press it carefully into each crevice.

PREBAKING THE CRUST Line the crust (bottom and sides) with greased aluminum foil or parchment paper and fill the shell with baking beans or rice so that the weights fill at least one half of the shell. The weights will keep the crust from puffing up as it bakes. Place the shell in the refrigerator for 30 minutes to relax the dough and chill the butter.

While the shell is chilling, preheat the oven to 350°F. When ready, bake the shell for 15 minutes, then remove the foil and beans and continue baking for about 12 minutes more or until the crust is light golden brown. Cool completely before filling.

Opposite: Chocolate Cream Pie (page 24).
Page following: New York Lime Pie (page 26).

LATTICE-TOP APPLE PIE

SERVES 8

INGREDIENTS

*1 batch Flaky Pie Crust
    dough*

*5 medium apples,
    preferably tart ones such
    as Granny Smiths*

¼ cup (½ stick) butter

½ cup dark brown sugar

*1 to 2 tablespoons ground
    cinnamon*

¼ teaspoon grated nutmeg

¼ teaspoon salt

¼ cup raisins (optional)

*¼ cup chopped nuts
    (optional)*

Juice of 1 lemon (optional)

1 While the dough is chilling in the refrigerator, prepare the apple pie filling. Peel and slice the apples not too thinly—about ¼ inch thick. Place the slices immediately into a large saucepan with the butter and sugar. Add the spices and cook filling over medium-low heat for a few minutes. In no more than 5 minutes, the apple slices should be swimming in juice and slightly soft. Do not overcook, or the apples will get too soft and bland when later baked in the pie. Cooking the apples at this point allows for less shrinkage in the oven, yielding ultimately a denser, more firmly packed and attractive filling for the pie. Add the raisins, nuts, or lemon juice, if desired.

2 When the filling has cooked, place it in a bowl to cool while you roll out the pie crust. Use about ⅔s of the dough for the lattice top, reserving only ⅓ for the bottom crust. Take that ⅓ of chilled dough and shape it roughly into a disc, then roll it out onto a floured surface until ⅛ inch thick and about 12 inches in diameter. Lift the dough off the counter and use it to line the bottom of an 8-inch pie pan. Note: Flaky pie crust should not be over-worked but you can get a head start toward the circle for the crust by holding the dough in your hands and shaping it into a circle. Also, by preshaping the dough, you'll be left with fewer scraps. When you bake a pie with a filling in it, the filling does not allow the crust to flake up very much. This means that, for this pie, you must roll the crust very thin in order to bake it crisp.

3 Pour the filling into the shell and spread out to fill completely.

4 Carefully roll out the remaining ⅔s of dough into a rectangle that measures about 10 by 12 inches, or large enough to cut 18 or 20 strips each about ½ inch wide. Use a pastry wheel to cut the strips, then arrange half the strips across the apple filling. Sifting each alternate strip, weave the remaining ones over and under the first ones. Don't weave the lattice strips perpendicular to one another. Instead, weave them in at an angle, forming diamond shapes, since these are more pleasing to the eye than squares.

Crimp together the lattice strips and bottom crust, making them look like one continuous piece of dough. Chill the pie for at least 30 minutes.

5 Preheat the oven to 350°F. Bake the pie for about 45 minutes, or until the crust is light golden brown all over. Cool for at least 30 minutes before slicing. Accompany slices with a dollop of whipped cream or a scoop of vanilla ice cream, "a la mode."

OLD FASHIONED PUMPKIN PIE

SERVES 8

INGREDIENTS

½ batch Flaky Pie Crust
   dough
2 large eggs
⅓ cup dark brown sugar
⅓ cup granulated sugar
¼ teaspoon salt
1 to 2 tablespoons ground
   cinnamon
Pinch of grated nutmeg
Pinch of ground ginger
1 can (16 ounces)
   pumpkin puree
1½ cups half and half
1 teaspoon vanilla extract

Reasonably priced pumpkins abound each autumn in certain parts of the country, especially New England, making pumpkin pie a historical favorite around Thanksgiving and Christmas. Nevertheless, in this recipe I use canned pumpkin puree, which is available all year long and also a lot easier than butchering a fresh pumpkin.

1 Roll out the dough to fill a 9-inch pie pan. Chill dough in pan for at least 30 minutes, or longer. While the dough chills, prepare the filling and preheat oven to 350°F.

2 In a large bowl, combine the eggs, sugars, salt, spices, pumpkin puree, half and half, and vanilla; mix well. Pour mixture into the pie shell and bake for about 50 minutes, or until set in the center. Don't overbake the pie. The filling continues to set after you remove the pie from the oven. Serve alone or with whipped cream.

NOTE   Don't substitute canned pumpkin pie filling; check the label carefully.

Pumpkin pie does not reheat well and is best served chilled. It can be stored in the refrigerator for several days.

CHOCOLATE CREAM PIE

Photo opposite page 20

SERVES 8

INGREDIENTS

½ *batch Flaky Pie Crust dough*

1 cup milk

½ *cup + 1 tablespoon granulated sugar*

3 large egg yolks

Pinch of salt

¼ *cup all-purpose flour*

1 tablespoon vanilla extract

1 tablespoon butter

2 ounces semisweet chocolate, chopped fine

1 cup heavy cream

This is one of my favorite pies because it is so simple, so beautiful, and so delicious, too. The flaky crust blends perfectly with the luscious chocolate custard and light vanilla whipped cream. Chocolate curls give a tasty and striking finish.

1 Roll out the dough for the pie shell and place in an 8-inch pie pan. Line the shell with greased aluminum foil and fill with baking beans or weights. Chill for 30 minutes, then bake at 350°F. for 15 minutes. Remove foil and weights and continue baking for additional 12 minutes or until crust is light golden brown. Let cool completely.

2 Meanwhile, prepare the filling. Heat the milk with ¼ cup of the sugar in a heavy stainless-steel or enamel pot. Whisk the sugar with the milk until it dissolves. Keep warm while you beat the yolks and ¼ sugar in a mixing bowl. Add the salt and 2 teaspoons vanilla and mix until smooth. Add the flour slowly, whisking it into the yolk mixture.

3 Bring the milk to a rolling boil, then whisk about ⅓ of it into the yolk mixture to temper it. Bring the remaining ⅔s of the milk mixture back to a rolling boil over medium heat and whisk in the tempered yolk mixture. Don't stop whisking, or lumps will form.

4 Place the butter in the bottom of a cool mixing bowl and have it ready for the custard. When the custard begins to boil and the flour in it is cooked, add the chopped chocolate and stir to melt the chocolate into the custard. Pour the hot chocolate custard mixture onto the butter in the bowl and whisk butter into the custard until it melts. Cover custard with plastic wrap and chill for at least 1 hour.

5 Whip together the heavy cream, remaining 1 tablespoon sugar, and remaining 1 teaspoon vanilla until cream forms firm peaks.

6 Spread cooled chocolate custard into cooled pie shell. Fit a pastry bag with a no. 6 star tip and fill bag with whipped cream. Pipe *fleurettes* onto the pie using as much of the whipped cream as desired. Garnish with chocolate curls or sprinkles.

NOTE The components for this dessert can easily be prepared ahead and then assembled on a moment's notice, ensuring that flavors and textures are perfect.

NEW YORK LIME PIE

Photo 2 following page 20

SERVES 6 TO 8

INGREDIENTS

½ *batch Flaky Pie Crust dough*

6 large egg yolks

1 cup granulated sugar

Juice and zest of 3 ripe limes

Zest of 1 lemon

½ *cup (1 stick) butter, in pieces*

Pinch of salt (optional)

8 ounces cream cheese, at room temperature

This summertime favorite is pretty and just a bit tart. The lime filling is easy and quick.

1 Roll out the dough for the pie shell and place in an 8-inch pie pan. Line the shell with greased aluminum foil and fill with baking beans or weights. Chill for 30 minutes, then bake at 350°F. for 15 minutes. Remove foil and weights and continue baking for an additional 12 minutes or until crust is light golden brown. Let cool completely.

2 In a large stainless-steel pot set over low heat, slowly whisk the egg yolks with the sugar for a couple of minutes or until sugar melts into the eggs. Then add the lime juice and zest, the lemon zest, and the butter in pieces. Add the salt, if desired, and stir over low heat until the mixture thickens and starts to boil. Immediately remove from heat and strain.

3 Pour lime filling into the prepared shell and bake the pie for about 40 minutes, or until the filling is almost fully set. Remember, it will set further as it cools.

4 Prepare the decorative topping. Whip the cream cheese until light and fluffy. Fit a pastry bag with a no. 6 star tip, then fill with the cream cheese and pipe a series of *fleurettes* around the edge of the pie. Serve chilled.

NOTE   Don't use an aluminum pot to cool the filling; it will react with the acidic fruit and discolor the filling.

The components for this recipe can be prepared ahead and assembled and decorated in just a few minutes. The filling can also be used as a base for many other pastries, soufflés, mousses, or even buttercream frosting.

As an alternative, the filling can become a lemon or orange pie just by substituting fruits.

LEMON MERINGUE PIE

INGREDIENTS

½ batch Flaky Pie Crust
  dough
1 cup milk
½ cup granulated sugar
3 large egg yolks
¼ cup all-purpose flour
Pinch of salt
Juice of 1 lemon
Zest of 2 lemons
1 tablespoon butter

MERINGUE TOPPING

4 large egg whites (about
  ½ cup)
Pinch of salt
1 cup granulated sugar

This pie is filled with a smooth lemon filling and topped with Swiss meringue.

1 Roll out the dough for the pie shell and place in a 9-inch pie pan. Line the shell with greased aluminum foil and fill with baking beans or weights. Chill for 30 minutes, then bake at 350°F. for 15 minutes. Remove foil and weights and continue baking for an additional 12 minutes or until crust is light golden brown. Let cool completely.

2 In a large stainless-steel pot over low heat, bring the milk and half the sugar to a boil. Whisk together the egg yolks with the remaining sugar, then slowly whisk in the flour. Beat a little of the hot milk into this paste to temper it, then pour the tempered paste into the milk mixture. Add the salt, lemon juice, and lemon zest. Whisk steadily while you bring the mixture back to a boil. Cook on medium heat for at least 30 seconds (to cook the flour). Place the butter in the bottom of a mixing bowl, and then pour the custard directly through a strainer onto the butter. Whisk to blend the butter with the milk, then cover the

custard with plastic wrap, pressing the plastic directly onto the custard to keep a skin from forming. Refrigerate for at least 45 minutes.

3 Prepare the meringue by beating the egg whites and salt until they form soft peaks, then gradually add the sugar, one tablespoon at a time, until they form stiff peaks.

4 Spread the custard in the pie shell. Fill a pastry bag with the meringue and pipe it directly onto the custard. Place the pie at least 5 inches from the heat of your broiler, and brown the meringue just a bit. Watch the meringue; this browning should take no more than a few seconds!

MAPLE PECAN PIE

Photo 3 following page 20

SERVES 8

INGREDIENTS

½ batch Flaky Pie Crust
  dough
3 large eggs
½ cup brown sugar
½ cup granulated sugar
2 teaspoons vanilla extract
½ cup light corn syrup
¼ cup natural maple syrup
¼ teaspoon salt
1 cup pecan halves, lightly
  toasted

Fast and easy, this pie only uses one ingredient that you might not have around the house—pecans. Maple syrup has been used in place of more sugar or corn syrup; it really brings out the flavor of the pecans.

1 Roll out the dough on a floured surface until about ⅛ inch thick, then use to line a 9-inch pie pan. Chill dough for 30 minutes. Preheat oven to 350°F.

2 In a large bowl, combine the eggs, brown sugar, granulated sugar, vanilla, syrups, and salt. Mix well, then add the pecans.

3 Pour nut mixture into the prebaked pie shell and bake for about 40 minutes or until filling is moderately firm. The filling does not quite set, but should hold together. It will settle further and set as it cools. Let pie cool on a rack, and serve at room temperature or slightly warm, alone or accompanied by whipped cream.

PEACH PIE IN A WHOLE-WHEAT CRUST

INGREDIENTS

5 ripe medium peaches
1 cup granulated sugar
1 tablespoon ground
  cinnamon
Pinch of grated nutmeg
½ cup (1 stick) butter,
  diced

CRUST

1 cup whole-wheat flour
1 cup all-purpose flour
1 teaspoon salt
⅔ cup butter
⅓ cup cold water

1 Prepare the crust. In a large mixing bowl, mix the flours and salt. Cut in the butter and mix until butter pieces are the size of raisins. Then add the cold water and mix dough until it holds together in one piece but is still coarse and marblized. Do not over-mix. Chill for at least 45 minutes.

2 Meanwhile, prepare the filling. Slice and pit the peaches (don't peel them). Toss the slices with the remaining ingredients in a bowl and leave for about 30 minutes.

3 Divide the pie crust dough in half and roll out each half to a circle about 10 inches wide and ⅛ inch thick. Line an 8-inch pie pan with one circle, then fill shell with the peach mixture. Cover with top circle and crimp edges together. Cut a vent hole in the top, using a decorative pattern such as a half moon. Chill pie for at least 30 minutes before baking.

4 Preheat the oven to 350°F., then bake pie for about 40 minutes, or until slightly browned. Let cool for 30 minutes then serve warm.

PEACH ALMOND TART

INGREDIENTS

½ cup (1 stick) butter
¼ pound almond paste
½ cup granulated sugar
2 large eggs
¼ cup all-purpose flour
4 to 5 firm, medium
    peaches
½ cup apricot preserves
2 tablespoons water
¼ cup sliced almonds,
    toasted

SWEET FLAKY CRUST

1½ cups flour
Pinch of salt
1 tablespoon granulated
    sugar
½ cup butter, in pieces
1 tablespoon very cold
    water

This is perfect during peach season, or anytime ripe fresh peaches are available. The fruit and nuts make a delicious blend of flavors and textures.

1 First prepare the crust. Sift together the flour, salt, and sugar into a large bowl. Cut in the butter, using your fingertips, until the mixture resembles cornmeal in texture. Make a well in the center and add the water, then mix together with the flour to form a firm dough. Don't over-mix; work dough just until it holds together. Wrap dough in plastic, then let rest in refrigerator for 15 minutes before rolling out.

2 While the dough is chilling, prepare the filling. In a large bowl, beat together the butter and almond paste until the mixture is smooth. Add the sugar and beat the mixture until it is fluffy. Beat in the eggs, one at a time, then stir in the flour. Don't over-mix; just blend until smooth.

3 Preheat the oven to 350°F. Roll out the dough onto a floured surface to form a circle large enough to line an 8-inch tart pan—about 10 inches in diameter. Fit the dough into

the pan snugly, then trim away the excess dough by rolling your rolling pin over the top of the tart pan.

4 Fill the shell with the almond mixture, making a smooth layer on the bottom. Bake filled shell for about 25 minutes, or until just set. Let cool.

5 Meanwhile, prepare the peaches by making a small X on the bottom of each peach. Plunge the peaches into boiling water for about 30 seconds, then quickly remove and plunge into very cold water. Remove the skins from the peaches, then cut peaches in half and pit them.

6 Arrange the peach halves on the cooled pastry. Heat the apricot preserves and water in a small saucepan set over low heat, then strain to remove solids. Brush the peaches with the apricot glaze and spinkle the top of the tart with toasted almonds. Chill for 30 minutes before serving.

CARAMELIZED PEAR TART

SERVES 8

INGREDIENTS

¾ *cup granulated sugar*
Juice of 1 lemon
3 tablespoons butter, in
  pieces
5 large, firm pears
½ *batch Flaky Pie Crust*
  dough

A variation on the classic *tarte tatin,* this is delicious anytime but makes a special winter treat. The pears need not be ripe.

1 Place the sugar and lemon juice in a 9-inch ovenproof skillet over medium heat and cook until sugar melts and dissolves with the lemon juice. Stir and continue to cool until the sugar caramelizes and turns dark brown. Remove from the heat and gently mix in the butter. Set aside briefly.

2 While the sugar caramelizes, peel the pears and quarter them. Slice the core off each quarter, leaving a flat spot on the bottom. Turn each quarter onto its flat spot and slice the pear quarters into ¼-inch slices *without* separating each quarter (see drawing). Place the pear quarters (without separating the slices) onto the caramelized sugar, flat side up.

3 Preheat the oven to 350°F.

4 While the caramelized sugar is cooling with the pears, roll out the pie crust to a 9-inch circle, or just large enough to cover the fruit and reach the rim of the pan. Place crust on top of skillet and then put skillet in oven and bake for about 20 minutes, or just until the crust browns.

5 Invert a 10-inch plate over the crust and quickly turn the entire tart over, before the sugar has hardened. Be very careful not to allow the cooked sugar to drip onto your hands. Turn the plate in one quick motion for the neatest results. This tart is best served fresh and warm from the oven, but it also keeps well in the refrigerator and reheats beautifully.

STRAWBERRY CUSTARD TART

SERVES 10

INGREDIENTS

1 batch Flaky Pie Crust dough

2 cups milk

¾ cup granulated sugar

6 egg yolks

Pinch of salt

1½ teaspoons vanilla extract

⅓ cup all-purpose flour

2 tablespoons butter

½ cup apricot preserves

1 tablespoon water or liqueur (optional)

2 pints fresh strawberries

1 Roll out the dough for the pie shell and place in a 10-inch pie pan. Line the shell with greased aluminum foil and fill with baking beans or weights. Chill for 30 minutes, then bake at 350°F. for 15 minutes. Remove foil and weights and continue baking for an additional 12 minutes or until crust is light golden brown. Let cool completely.

2 Heat the milk with half the sugar in a heavy stainless steel or enamel pot. (Don't use aluminum because it will react with the ingredients and cause a greenish tinge.) Whisk the sugar with the milk until it dissolves. Keep warm.

3 Beat together the yolks and the remaining sugar in a large mixing bowl. Then add the salt and vanilla and mix until smooth. Add the flour slowly, whisking it in.

4 Bring the milk to a rolling boil, then whisk about ⅓ of it into the yolk mixture to temper it. Bring the remaining ⅔s of the milk mixture back to a rolling boil over medium heat and whisk in the tempered yolk mixture.

Opposite: Strawberry Custard Tart.

5 Place the butter in the bottom of a cool mixing bowl and have it ready for the custard. When the custard begins to boil and the flour in it is cooked (you will notice a perking on the surface), immediately pour the custard through a sieve onto the butter in the bowl. Whisk the butter into the custard until it melts, then cover the custard with plastic wrap, pressing the plastic lightly onto the surface of the custard. Chill for 1 hour.

6 Bring the preserves to a boil in a small saucepan. If the preserves seem too thick, add the water or liqueur. Strain the preserves and set aside.

7 Trim the stems and hulls from the strawberries, then cut the berries in half from stem to blossom end.

8 To assemble the tart, spread the cooled custard across the crust to a thickness of about ¼ inch. (Note: You won't need to use all the custard and if you do attempt to use it all, the layer will be too thick. To make a smaller batch of custard is difficult to mix and temper smooth, so you are best preparing more custard filling than you need and reserving the rest for another dessert.)

9 Arrange the sliced berries piggy-back style in concentric circles, pressing them lightly into the custard. Brush the finished tart, including the crust, with the apricot preserves and serve at once.

Opposite: Miniature Fruit Tarts. (page 44).

BANANA CREAM TART

SERVES 6 TO 8

INGREDIENTS

½ batch Flaky Pie Crust
  dough
1 cup milk
½ cup + 1 teaspoon
  granulated sugar
3 large egg yolks
Pinch of salt
1½ teaspoons vanilla
  extract
2 ripe bananas, 1 mashed
  and 1 in ¼-inch slices
¼ cup all-purpose flour
1 tablespoon butter
1 cup heavy cream

1 Roll out the dough for the pie shell and place in a 9-inch tart pan. Line the shell with greased aluminum foil and fill with baking beans or weights. Chill for 30 minutes, then bake at 350°F. for 15 minutes. Remove foil and weights and continue baking for an additional 12 minutes or until crust is light golden brown. Let cool completely.

2 In a large stainless-steel pot set over low heat, bring the milk and ¼ cup of sugar to a boil. Whisk together the yolks, salt, 1 teaspoon vanilla, and mashed banana with ¼ cup sugar, then slowly whisk in the flour. Beat a little of the boiling milk into this paste to temper it, then pour the tempered paste into the milk, whisking constantly. When the custard returns to a boil, let it simmer for at least 30 seconds to 1 minute, so as to cook the flour. Place the butter in the bottom of a bowl and then pour the custard through the strainer into the bowl. Whisk the butter into the custard. Cover the custard with plastic wrap, pressing the wrap down onto the custard surface; this keeps a skin from forming. Chill for at least 45 minutes.

3 Whip the cream with the remaining tablespoon of sugar and remaining ½ teaspoon of vanilla. Set aside.

4 Spread the custard in the tart shell and arrange the sliced banana over the top. Cover the entire tart with rosettes of whipped cream, then chill for at least 1 hour before serving.

THREE-NUT CHOCOLATE TART

INGREDIENTS

*½ batch Flaky Pie Crust
   dough*
½ cup walnut pieces
½ cup sliced almonds
½ cup pecan pieces
1 tablespoon honey
¾ cup heavy cream
1½ cups granulated sugar
Pinch of cream of tartar
½ cup water

CHOCOLATE GLAZE

*4 ounces semisweet
   chocolate, chopped fine*
⅓ cup heavy cream
1 tablespoon butter
1 teaspoon vanilla extract

1 Preheat oven to 350°F. Roll out dough until ¼ inch thick and use to line an 8-inch tart pan. Line the shell with greased aluminum foil, fill with dried beans or weights, and bake for 15 minutes. Remove foil and weights and bake for 10 minutes more. Remove shell from the oven and let cool. Keep oven at 350°F.

2 Toast the nuts on a cookie sheet in the oven for about 6 minutes, or until light brown. Remove from oven and let cool.

3 Mix the honey and cream in a bowl and set aside. Place the sugar, cream of tartar, and water in a heavy-bottomed saucepan and cook over low heat until the mixture forms a light brown caramel. Remove pan from heat and carefully stir in the honey-cream mixture. Return pan to the heat and bring mixture to a boil. Boil without stirring until the mixture reaches 240°F. on a candy thermometer, or soft-ball stage. Stir in the toasted nuts and then spoon the mixture evenly into the tart shell. Set aside.

4 Prepare the glaze. Place the chocolate, cream, and butter in a heavy-bottomed saucepan and cook over medium heat until the chocolate has melted. Stir gently. Add the vanilla and let mixture cool to room temperature. When cooled, spread evenly over nut tart and chill to set the chocolate. Serve tart at room temperature.

LINZER TART

INGREDIENTS

1 cup (2 sticks) butter
1 cup granulated sugar
1 large egg
½ teaspoon vanilla extract
*1 teaspoon grated orange
  rind*
1½ cups all-purpose flour
1 cup ground hazelnuts
½ cup ground almonds
*1 teaspoon ground
  cinnamon*
½ teaspoon baking powder
½ teaspoon salt
1 cup raspberry preserves
Confectioners sugar

1 Cream together butter and sugar until light and fluffy. Mix in egg, vanilla, and orange rind. Combine flour with ground nuts, cinnamon, baking powder, and salt; add to butter mixture, mixing until the dough holds together. Divide dough into 2 equal portions and chill for 1 hour.

2 Roll out ¾s of one portion of dough until it is ¼ inch thick. Use dough to line an 8-inch tart pan. Spread ⅓ cup preserves on top. Roll ¾s of the second portion of dough until ¼ inch thick; place dough over layer of preserves; trim edges as necessary. Spread with another ⅓ cup of preserves. With the remaining dough pieces, roll out an 8 by 10-inch rectangle and cut eight 1-inch strips for a lattice top. Place the strips on top of the preserves layer, crossing them diagonally to form a diamond pattern. Chill tart for 15 minutes.

3 Preheat the oven to 350°F. Bake the tart for 25 to 30 minutes, or until lightly browned on top. Cool completely, then sift confectioners sugar over the top. With the remaining ⅓ cup preserves, fill in the diamond spaces between strips.

SOUR CREAM CHERRY TART WITH SUGAR COOKIE CRUST

INGREDIENTS

2 large eggs, lightly beaten
1 cup sour cream
½ cup granulated sugar
1 teaspoon vanilla
1 pound pitted sweet
  cherries

COOKIE CRUST

1 cup (2 sticks) butter
⅔ cup granulated sugar
1 large egg
2 cups all-purpose flour
½ teaspoon salt

1 Prepare the crust. Beat together the butter and sugar until creamy. Add the egg and mix well. Add the flour and salt, and mix by hand until the dough holds together. Chill for 1 hour.

2 Mix the eggs with the sour cream, sugar, and vanilla. Whisk in the egg and set aside.

3 Preheat the oven to 350°F.

4 Roll out the cookie crust until ¼ inch thick. Use the crust to line an 8-inch tart pan. Place the cherries into the shell, distributing them evenly over the bottom. Pour in the sour cream mixture and bake tart for about 20 to 25 minutes, or until custard has set. Let cool before serving.

MINIATURE FRUIT TARTS

Photo opposite page 37

SERVES 12

INGREDIENTS

½ *batch Flaky Pie Crust dough*

1 *quart assorted fresh fruits, small ones left whole and large ones sliced*

2 *cups milk*

¾ *cup granulated sugar*

6 *egg yolks*

Pinch of salt

1½ *teaspoons vanilla extract*

⅓ *cup all-purpose flour*

2 *tablespoons butter*

½ *cup red currant jelly*

1 *tablespoon water*

These little gems are both mouth-watering and dazzling. They're also fun to eat. Keep them simple and elegant.

1 Preheat the oven to 350°F. Roll out the dough just a little thinner than for larger pies, about ⅛ to 1/16 inch thick. Cut pieces of dough to line the bottoms of about 12 miniature tart pans—ovals, circles, barquettes, and so on. Place a greased empty tart pan inside of each to hold the dough in place and prevent excess puffing while they bake (or line with greased aluminum foil and baking weights). Bake the tart crusts together on 1 baking sheet for about 10 minutes. Remove the empty pans or baking weights and foil and bake shells for another couple of minutes, or until light golden brown. Let cool completely.

2 Prepare the pastry cream. Heat the milk with half the sugar in a heavy stainless-steel or enamel pan. Whisk the sugar with the milk until it dissolves. Keep warm.

3 Beat together the yolks and the remaining sugar in a large mixing bowl. Then add the salt and vanilla and mix until smooth. Add the flour slowly, whisking it into the yolk mixture. Bring the milk to a rolling boil, then whisk about ⅓ of it into the yolk mixture to temper it. Bring the remaining ⅔s of the milk mixture back to a rolling boil over medium heat and whisk in the tempered yolk mixture. Don't stop whisking as the custard thickens, lest it begin to lump up. Remove pot from the heat and whisk in the butter. Chill for about 1 hour.

4 Smooth a thin layer of pastry cream into the bottom of each tart shell. (Note: you will have pastry cream left over; use it for another recipe.) Add a row of sliced or whole small fruits.

5 Melt the jelly with the water in a small saucepan over medium heat until dissolved. Brush each of the tarts with the glaze, then chill for 30 minutes before serving.

NOTE These tarts can also be topped with toasted slivered almonds, for a different effect.

INDIVIDUAL DEEP-DISH
APPLE PIES

SERVES 5

INGREDIENTS

5 large apples, peeled, cored, and sliced

½ cup dark brown sugar

1 cup (2 sticks) butter, in pieces

2 tablespoons ground cinnamon

¼ teaspoon grated nutmeg

1 batch Flaky Pie Crust dough

1 large egg, lightly beaten

1 Place the apple slices, sugar, butter, and spices in a large saucepan and cook over medium heat for about 5 minutes, or until the mixture is juicy; do not over-cook.

2 Preheat the oven to 350°F. Roll out the dough onto a floured surface until ⅛ inch thick. Cut out circles of dough about 6 inches in diameter, or large enough to cover ramekins.

3 Place a portion of filling into each ramekin, then brush the edges with some beaten egg. Cover each ramekin with a circle of dough and cut a slit in the top of each to allow steam to escape. Use the scraps of dough that remain to make decorations for the tops and attach to the top crust with some beaten egg.

4 Glaze the tops with the remaining beaten egg, and put the ramekins on a baking sheet. Bake for about 20 to 25 minutes, or until the juices from the apples start to bubble up through the steam vents and the crusts are golden brown. Let cool slightly and then serve warm or at room temperature.

PUFF PASTRIES

Puff pastry is the richest and most elegant of pastry doughs. Hundreds of paper-thin layers of butter releasing steam all at once can raise this dough four to six times its original size as it bakes. The power of steam is formidable (locomotives used to run on it, after all). It is just this dramatic leavening process that makes puff pastry exciting and rewarding.

Don't be intimidated by instructions that may at first seem forbidding. With a bit of determination and practice, even the beginner can make a tender, flaky, and buttery puff pastry. Most important, keep yourself and your dough cool and relaxed. During warm weather, try to turn the dough early in the morning, before the day's heat has set in.

Puff pastry is not nearly as laborious as you may have thought. Most of the time is spent waiting in between turns of the dough, and that resting time frees you to do other things. A common home-baker's mistake is rushing the cold butter into a soft dough. Remember that the butter must be as soft as the dough. Don't be afraid to work it well with flour, since it will not begin to melt until it reaches a temperature of 80°F.

Puff pastry is perfect for desserts, appetizers, and even main courses (for example, beef Wellington). There is no reason why you shouldn't experiment with your own shapes and combinations. Homemade puff pastry costs only about $1 a pound, while the store-bought frozen kind (which is never as good) costs four or five times as much. Make a large batch of puff pastry all at once, and then freeze smaller blocks to be thawed overnight and used the next day. The effort is well worth it.

PUFF PASTRY DOUGH

INGREDIENTS

*4 cups all-purpose flour,
    approximately*
*2 teaspoons granulated
    sugar*
2 teaspoons salt
1¼ cups milk, very cold
1 pound butter, very cold

1 In a large bowl, mix 3⅓ cups of the flour with the sugar and salt. Add the milk and begin tossing with the flour. Smear the flour and milk along the sides of the bowl to blend well, then incorporate into the mixture. If the moisture is absorbed too quickly by the flour, add another tablespoon or so of cold milk. Mix well, but do not over-work the dough or knead it. If it seems heavy, add just a little more milk to get a dough that is still very soft. Sprinkle a pinch of flour over it and then flatten the dough. It should look coarse and marblized but hold together in one piece. Cover with plastic wrap and refrigerate while you prepare the butter.

2 Clear the work area and then pour on the remaining ⅔ cup flour. Remove the butter from the refrigerator and place onto the flour. Keep the butter covered with the flour while cutting and kneading it quickly with a pastry scraper. Feel for cold lumps in the butter, which might later damage the layers; break them up and blend with the flour. Add a bit more flour, if necessary, to properly soften the butter without melting it. Once the butter is soft but not melted, and thoroughly dusted all around, form it into a rough square.

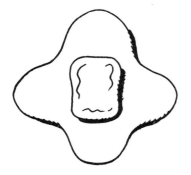

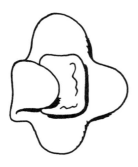

3 Scrape down the work area again and toss on some fresh flour. Place the chilled dough onto the flour without folding or handling it too much. Roll out the dough corners into thin flaps, which you will use to enclose the softened butter. Place the softened square of butter onto the dough as shown in the drawing. Lift each flap snugly over the butter, making sure to overlap the corners and seal up the bundle.

4 The dough package is now ready for the first of 4 double turns, or folds. This dough-butter bundle will be stretched into about 260 layers, and ideally the butter is spread to an even thickness equally distributed across each successive layer. Here are a few tips before actually beginning with the turns: 1. Keep the dough separate from the work surface by frequent rotations and adequate flouring. 2. Leave the center of the dough thicker by rolling away from it. 3. If you put more pressure on the rolling pin, you'll have fewer repeated rolls over the dough and the resulting dough will require less work and be easier to handle. 4. Keep a good pastry scraper and a bowl of clean flour handy at all times.

5 Assuming your kitchen is cool (below 72°F.) and the butter has not begun to melt, you need not be in a rush to complete this first and most critical turn. Start by pounding the dough gently in one direction. If you begin rolling, make sure the dough is not stuck to the work surface. Roll only in one direction and not past the far end. Rolling past the end will pinch

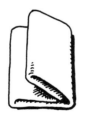

and smear the layers at the edge. Roll and manipulate the dough into a rectangle about 20 inches long and 8 inches wide. Press hard on the handles of the rolling pin to form the rectangle, then brush off any excess flour from the surface of the dough. Bring both ends toward the center like a book, leaving a small space in between for the spine. Fold in half, "closing" your book. Wrap the pastry dough in plastic and refrigerate it for at least 45 minutes. Your dough has been turned once, and it now has 4 layers.

6 Place the chilled and rested dough on a lightly floured surface so that the spine of your book becomes the long side of your rectangle. Begin again by pounding gently. If the edges crack slightly, take your time working the dough and don't get upset. This time the dough should be chilled and relaxed enough to turn twice without a rest in between. Make your next rectangle large, about 12 by 18 inches. This will not only make turn no. 3 easier but will help ensure equal and smooth distribution of butter between the layers. Fold and turn in the same way as before, first forming a rectangle that measures about 10 by 14 inches, then folding the 2 sides into the center with a gap in the middle for the "spine." Fold in half, making sure the "spine" of your book becomes the length of the rectangle. Rest the dough after turn no. 3 for about 1 hour in the refrigerator.

Opposite: Braided Fruit Strip (page 63).
Page following: Apple Puffs (page 57).

7 The fourth and final turn should reveal the dough to be smooth and just a bit elastic. Try to form well-defined corners and neat edges to your rectangle. Fold and turn once more in the same way, then chill for at least 4 or 5 hours before using.

NOTE   You may have to vary the amounts of butter, flour, or milk slightly in order to achieve the desired texture. This is a common practice, since there are so many variables in making puff pastry and because flours differ substantially in their ability to absorb moisture. It is more important to manipulate the components quickly to reach the proper consistency than to adhere to exact measurements. Trust your instincts and practice until you have what works for you.

Puff pastry freezes wonderfully and is easily thawed in the refrigerator overnight before using in a recipe.

Opposite: Sweet Cinnamon Straws and
Palmiers (pages 54 and 55).
Page preceding: Cream Horns (page 60).

SWEET CINNAMON STRAWS

Photo opposite page 53

MAKES ABOUT TWENTY 8-INCH STRAWS

INGREDIENTS

½ cup granulated sugar
1 tablespoon ground cinnamon
½ pound Puff Pastry Dough

1 In a bowl, mix the sugar with the cinnamon. Dust the work surface generously with the cinnamon sugar and also dust the dough with some of the sugar.

2 Roll out dough to an 8-inch square. Scrape it up and rotate it regularly, dusting all the while with sugar. Roll it to an even ⅛-inch thickness: not too thin or some portion of the layers will be damaged, and not too thick or you'll have trouble baking through the dough without burning the outside. Sprinkle with more cinnamon sugar. Puff pastry expands but the coating will not, so use more than you would think necessary.

3 Cut strips about ½ inch wide, using a pastry wheel, and then twist strips into straws. Roll in 2 directions at the same time using both hands, as shown. Place the straws about 1 inch apart on a parchment-lined or lightly greased baking sheet. Chill the pastries for at least 30 minutes.

4 Preheat the oven to 350°F. Bake straws for about 12 minutes, or until they are browned and lightly crisp. Allow to cool for at least 15 minutes before serving.

PALMIERS

Photo opposite page 53

MAKES ABOUT 15

INGREDIENTS

½ cup granulated sugar
½ pound Puff Pastry Dough

Also called Angel Wings or Elephant Ears, these popular cookies have become an American favorite. Try a bit of cinnamon with the sugar for another pretty variation.

1 Dust the work surface with sugar and also dust the square of puff pastry. Roll out the dough to an 8-inch square. Scrape up dough and rotate it regularly while dusting with sugar. Roll to an even ⅛-inch thickness, not too thin in spots and not too thick. Sprinkle with more sugar.

2 Trim away the rough edges with a pastry wheel. Fold both ends of the square to the center as though you were turning the dough. Leave a slight space for the "spine" and close your book by folding the dough in half again, as shown.

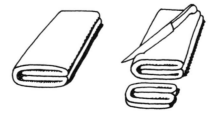

3 Slice the palmiers about ¼ inch thick and coat again in sugar. Place 2 inches apart on a lightly greased baking sheet or one lined with parchment paper. Chill for at least 20 minutes.

4 Preheat the oven to 350°F. Bake palmiers for about 18 to 20 minutes, or until entirely browned. Allow to cool at least 15 minutes before serving.

NOTE   As with the Cinnamon Straws, these pastries can be frozen after shaping and then baked directly from the freezer. Wrap tightly for storage in the freezer.

APPLE PUFFS

Photo 2 following page 52

MAKES 6 PUFFS

INGREDIENTS

2 tablespoons butter

⅓ cup light brown sugar

2 large apples, peeled,
  cored, and sliced

1 tablespoon ground
  cinnamon

¼ teaspoon grated nutmeg

1 pound Puff Pastry Dough

2 large eggs, lightly beaten

These are a smaller variation on the classic *jalousie aux pommes.*

1 Melt the butter and brown sugar in a saucepan over medium heat. Add the apple slices and spices, and cook over medium-low heat for about 5 minutes, or only until the apples are juicy and hot. Cooking the apples to this point avoids their releasing too much juice when baked in the pastry and also eliminates their shrinking too much later on. Remove apple slices from the pan with a slotted spoon, leaving behind any juice, and allow to cool while you prepare the pastry.

2 Roll the dough out onto a floured surface into an 8 by 16-inch rectangle. Trim edges, then divide dough into 12 squares, using a pastry wheel. Place about 1 tablespoon of filling on each of the centers of 6 squares, leaving enough room for the egg glaze to be brushed on around the filling. Brush the edges of each square with beaten egg, and cover each with one of the plain squares. Slit the top of each square to allow steam to escape, and crimp the edges together with the back of a knife.

Place 2 inches apart on a large greased baking sheet and chill for at least 30 minutes.

3 Preheat the oven to 350°F. Bake puffs for about 30 minutes, or until they are lightly browned and crisp. These are best served fresh and warm from the oven, although they can easily be frozen or refrigerated and reheated. Puff pastry always reheats beautifully.

RASPBERRY TURNOVERS

Photo opposite page 85

MAKES 8 TURNOVERS

INGREDIENTS

1 pound Puff Pastry Dough
1 cup raspberry preserves
2 large eggs, lightly beaten

1 Dust work surface lightly with flour; roll out the dough to a rectangle that measures 8 by 16 inches. Trim the edges, then cut the rectangle into 8 squares, each 4 inches.

2 Place about 2 teaspoons of raspberry preserves onto the center of each square; don't add too much or the filling might boil through the pastry. Brush the edges of each square with beaten egg, being careful not to let any glaze run down over the sides of the pastries. Bring the 2 opposite corners together to form a triangle and seal the filling by pressing the sides together without smearing the delicate flake of the dough. Slit the top of each turnover for steam to escape.

3 Transfer the pastries to a lightly greased baking sheet or sheet lined with parchment paper and place about 2 inches apart. Chill for about 30 minutes in the refrigerator.

4 Preheat the oven to 350°F. Bake the turnovers for 25 to 30 minutes, or until they are lightly browned and crisp. Let cool for 15 minutes before serving. As with Apple Puffs, these pastries are best enjoyed warm from the oven.

CREAM HORNS

Photo 3 following page 52

MAKES ABOUT 1 DOZEN

INGREDIENTS

1 pound Puff Pastry Dough
2 cups heavy cream
2 teaspoons granulated
* sugar*
1 teaspoon vanilla extract
Confectioners sugar

1 Roll out dough onto a lightly floured surface until you have a rectangle measuring about 10 by 16 inches and about ⅛ inch thick. Prick with a fork to prevent any unevenness. Cut into lengthwise strips 1 inch wide, using a pastry wheel.

2 Wrap each strip of dough around a well-greased cream horn mold or cannoli form, as shown (see photo). Be certain to keep the dough off the very ends of each form. Place the forms on a greased baking sheet about 3 inches apart, with the ends of the dough tucked underneath the forms. Press down. Chill the forms for 30 minutes.

3 Preheat the oven to 350°F. Bake horns for about 20 minutes, or until quite browned. Remove the molds and return the pastries to the oven to thoroughly dry the insides, about 5 additional minutes.

4 Whip the cream with the sugar and vanilla and then place in a large pastry bag fitted with a large plain tip. Pipe the cream into each of the horns and dust horns with confectioners sugar. Serve at once.

NAPOLEONS

Photo opposite page 84

MAKES 6 TO 8

INGREDIENTS

1 pound Puff Pastry Dough
2 cups heavy cream
2 teaspoons granulated
  sugar
1 teaspoon vanilla extract
Confectioners sugar

The ultimate combination of puff pastry and whipped cream, yet deceptively simple to construct.

1 Roll out dough onto a parchment paper-lined baking sheet to form a rectangle that measures 10 by 16 inches. You'll have to roll this pastry thinner than for many other puff pastries, about 1/16 inch thick. Prick dough with a fork to prevent unevenness and bubbling when it bakes. Chill in refrigerator (or a very cool place) for at least 30 minutes.

2 Preheat the oven to 350°F. Bake the puff pastry for at least 40 minutes, or until very brown and quite crispy. Let cool to room temperature, at least 45 minutes.

3 Trim the edges of the pastry with a sharp serrated knife. Rub the darker, crispier trimmings between your hands to make crumbs, then set aside. Divide the trimmed rectangle into 3 strips, cutting them lengthwise with a serrated knife.

4 Prepare the filling by whipping the cream with the sugar and vanilla until stiff.

5 Place 1 strip of pastry on your serving dish. Spread on about 1 cup of the whipped cream, then place on the second strip of pastry. Spread with remaining cream. Invert the remaining strip of pastry so that the flat side is on top of the cream. Press the reserved pastry crumbs around the sides, adhering them to the cream. Dust the top of the pastry with confectioners sugar and, if desired, score a design on top by heating a metal skewer until red hot and laying it on the confectioners sugar. To serve, cut the whole napoleon into individual pastries using a very sharp knife.

BRAIDED FRUIT STRIP

Photo opposite page 52

SERVES 8

INGREDIENTS

*½ pound Puff Pastry
Dough*

*1 quart assorted prepared
fresh fruit, such as
cherries, blackberries,
grapes, peaches, apricots,
kiwifruit*

1 large egg, lightly beaten

2 cups milk

¾ cup granulated sugar

6 large egg yolks

Pinch of salt

*1½ teaspoons vanilla
extract*

⅓ cup all-purpose flour

2 tablespoons butter

1 cup apricot preserves

1 tablespoon water

A delicious rainbow of fresh fruit, custard, and puff pastry.

1 Roll out pastry dough onto a floured surface to a large rectangle, about ⅛ inch thick. Trim edges to form a neat triangle about 6 by 12 inches, and use the trimmings to form 2 braids about 12 inches long, with 3 strands in each braid.

2 Transfer the pastry rectangle to a baking sheet and brush the edges with beaten egg. Place the braids down each of the longer sides and brush again with glaze. Prick the center of the strip with a fork to keep the pastry from bubbling up as it bakes. Chill pastry for at least 30 minutes.

3 Meanwhile, prepare the custard filling. Heat the milk with half the sugar in a heavy stainless-steel or enamel pot. Whisk the sugar with the milk until it dissolves. Keep warm. Beat together the yolks and remaining sugar in a large mixing bowl, then add the salt and vanilla and mix until smooth. Add the flour slowly, whisking it into the yolk mixture. Bring the milk to a rolling boil, then whisk about ⅓ of it into the yolk mixture to

temper it. Bring the remaining ⅔s of the milk mixture back to a rolling boil over medium heat and whisk in the tempered yolk mixture. Don't stop whisking the custard as it thickens, lest it lump up.

4 Place the butter in the bottom of a cool mixing bowl and have it ready for the custard. When the custard begins to boil and the flour in it is cooked, immediately pour the custard through a sieve onto the butter in the bowl. Whisk the butter into the custard until it melts, then cover the custard with plastic wrap, pressing the plastic lightly onto the surface of the custard. Let cool in refrigerator.

5 Preheat the oven to 350°F. Bake the pastry for about 40 minutes, or until it is well browned. Cool completely.

6 Fill the center of the strip with a thin layer of the filling, then arrange the fruits on top in rows. Melt the apricot preserves with the water in a small saucepan over low heat, then strain. Brush the tart with the glaze and trim the edges to make a neat finished tart. Chill for 30 minutes, then serve.

GATEAU PITHIVIERS

INGREDIENTS

1 pound Puff Pastry Dough
6 ounces almond paste
   (about ¾ cup)
½ cup (1 stick) butter
½ cup granulated sugar
Pinch of salt
1 large egg, lightly beaten

This classic French dessert is a must for almond lovers, and makes a striking presentation for guests.

1 Roll out dough onto a floured surface to form a rectangle that measures 8 × 16 inches and is about ⅛ to ¼ inch thick. Cut the rectangle in half and place one half on a lightly greased baking sheet.

2 Prepare the filling by creaming together the almond paste, butter, sugar, and salt until the mixture is smooth.

3 Place filling onto the dough and mound it in the center, leaving a 2-inch border around the edge. Brush the beaten egg all the way around, then place the other half of the dough over the filling.

4 Place a small bowl (about 6 inches in diameter at the rim) over the top of the pastry, covering the mound of filling but still leaving a 2-inch border. Press the bowl down so as to crease the dough but not cut through it. Trim the edge of the

dough into a circle following the bowl as a guide but still leaving the 2-inch border all around.

5 Drag the back of a knife into the dough up to the bowl's rim, making a crimped design all around the circle of dough, as shown. Remove the bowl carefully after crimping the edge. Cut a small steam vent in the top of the pastry and glaze the entire surface with beaten egg. Finish by scoring the mound at the center with a sharp knife, following a spiral design. Chill pastry for at least 30 minutes before baking.

6 Preheat the oven to 350°F. Bake the pastry for about 45 minutes or until well browned. Let cool for 30 minutes before serving.

NOTE To make a Chocolate Puff (photo opposite page 164), substitute 8 ounces of semisweet chocolate for the almond filling.

YEAST-RISEN PASTRIES

These pastries are grouped together here because they all are leavened with yeast. Some are traditional breakfast pastries, like croissants and brioche. Strictly speaking, these are neither breads nor desserts. Both are rich in butter, and in addition, croissants are also flaky because they are made with a turned dough. A typical continental breakfast would consist of a croissant or brioche, served with butter, preserves, and a pot of steaming coffee.

Other yeast-risen pastries are similar to croissants and brioche, especially the Kugelhopf because it is butter-rich and light. Kugelhopf, Pannetone, and Babka are enjoyed as holiday breads, afternoon snacks, and desserts. They are also sometimes eaten for breakfast. But regardless of the time of day, they are butter-rich and delicious.

Lastly, in this chapter you'll find the favorites Rum Baba and Savarin. These are two yeast-risen pastries that are thought of strictly as desserts. Enjoy them as you would any other sweet pastry, following a good meal or as an afternoon or late evening snack.

Opposite: Chocolate Croissants (page 75).

CROISSANTS

Croissants are a hybrid of bread and pastry. Croissant dough combines the chewiness and subtle fermentation of French bread with the richness and flakiness of puff pastry. The croissant falls into place somewhere between breads and desserts, not as flaky or buttery as puff pastry, nor as crusty or chewy as French bread.

This dough is not as forbidding as many would have you believe. Croissants are leavened by a combination of yeast and butter. Gases released by the dough give it it's characteristic flavor and raise it up, while steam released from the butter (which is about 15 percent water) makes it flaky and puffy. An understanding of these two actions is essential to making good croissants.

Yeast cells are unique among the leaveners, in that they are alive. These miraculous micro-organisms go through an entire life process, including the ingestion of food (carbohydrates) and subsequent release of waste gases (mostly carbon dioxide). Most important, they reproduce quite readily under the right conditions, enabling the baker to control the fermentation (flavor) and texture of the croissants. Temperature is the easiest way to manipulate yeast leavening. As the thermometer drops toward the freezing mark, production of gases slows down until actually stopping at 32°F. The cells begin to die in a colder environment, thus making the freezer undesirable for dough storage.

Yeast also dies when exposed to extreme heat—above 125°F. This fact makes refrigerators the ideal storage place for croissant dough, being cold enough to keep the dough for at least two or three days, but not cold enough to kill the yeast. Allowing the dough to rise for too long (even under refrigeration) will impart a strange fermented flavor to it. Older doughs are also more reluctant to properly rise again. Twelve to twenty-four hours seems to yield maximum results.

PAN-PROOFING This critical yet often overlooked procedure can make the difference between good croissants and excellent ones. Remember that yeast dies quickly in the extreme heat of an oven! Giving your finished shapes a head start (see recipe) on the sheet before baking enables the yeast to reproduce itself and activate before the oven ceases any activity. Ten to fifteen minutes is the maximum life expectancy for yeast in a 350° to 400°F. environment.

Before dying, however, the yeast does experience a burst of activity, making the final "jump" in the oven quite dramatic.

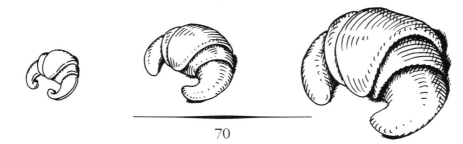

Short pan-proofing is one very common home maker's mistake. Under-baking is another. After much time and labor you will certainly be anxious to see some results. However, patience at these final stages will inevitably improve quality. An underbaked croissant is pale on the outside and "wet" on the inside. If this happens to you, put the croissants back into the oven until they improve. Bake them until they are a bit crispy.

At this point the croissants may be carefully sealed and frozen. They freeze beautifully. Simply place frozen croissants into a hot oven (375°F.) for about eight minutes and they will be almost as good as freshly made.

CROISSANT MADNESS A popular trend right now is to fill croissants with everything from spinach and cheese to sausage and eggs. Remember that croissants are delicate, flaky, and tender, with a subtle flavor all their own. They are quite rich and stand well by themselves, and thus in no way should be confused with a hero sandwich. They require patience and labor to create, and are well deserving of their own plate.

CLASSIC CROISSANTS

Photo opposite page 69

MAKES 12 TO 13

INGREDIENTS

4½ cups all-purpose flour
¼ cup granulated sugar
2 teaspoons salt
*1 envelope active dry yeast
  or ⅓ of a 1½-ounce
  cake*
1½ cups lukewarm water
¾ pound (3 sticks) butter
2 large eggs, lightly beaten

1 In a large bowl, mix 4 cups of the flour, the sugar, and the salt. Dissolve the yeast in the lukewarm water and add it to the dry ingredients. Mix only until you have a very soft, coarse consistency, about one minute. Don't over-mix or toughen the dough; it is better to add just a bit more water than to over-mix. The dough should be slightly sticky. Place it in a large greased bowl and cover. Chill for at least 3 to 4 hours. (Note: This basic croissant dough can also be risen at room temperature for about 1½ hours, however it is much easier to handle a chilled dough during the turning process. Chilling the dough also allows you to leave it in the refrigerator overnight, to be used any time the next day.)

2 Knead the remaining flour with the butter (as for puff pastry) and shape it into a 5-inch square. Dust with flour and move aside.

3 Remove the risen croissant dough carefully (without folding or over-working it) and drop it onto a well-floured surface. Roll a flap from each of the 4 corners (as for puff pastry) and wrap up the softened butter.

4 Croissants are turned 4 times, however each turn for this dough creates only *3* layers. Because of its softer nature, the croissant dough can be "book" turned (as shown below) 2 times at first. A one-hour rest is needed before the last 2 turns, however the dough will wait in the refrigerator, even overnight if desired. After 4 turns the croissant dough must be refrigerated at least 3 or 4 hours before using.

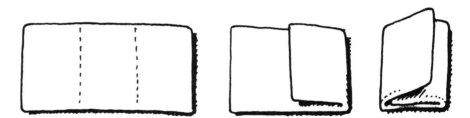

5 All or part of the dough may be rolled out for shaping. If making a dozen, roll to a rectangle that measures 21 by 7 or 8 inches and is ⅛ inch thick. Keep in mind that the triangular wedges to be shaped into croissants should be about 7 or 8 inches long and 3 inches across the base.

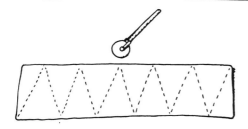 

6 Use a pastry wheel to cut the shapes. Trim all the edges before cutting. Croissants which are too small or too large don't bake through properly or have the same keeping qualities.

7 Place the croissant shapes on a lightly greased cookie sheet or on a sheet lined with parchment paper, leaving at least 2 inches between each one. Brush each with the beaten egg. Wait 30 minutes and glaze again.

8 Allow the finished shapes to rise one hour at room temperature, or until they are noticeably bigger. Don't allow the croissants to rise in too warm a spot.

9 Preheat oven to 350°F. Bake croissants for 30 minutes or until nicely browned.

CHOCOLATE CROISSANTS

Photo opposite page 68

MAKES 1 DOZEN

INGREDIENTS

*1 batch Classic Croissant
Dough*

*12 ounces semisweet
chocolate*

2 large eggs, lightly beaten

Called Pain au Chocolat, these are a favorite after-school snack for French children.

1 Roll out the dough to a rectangle that measures 8 by 15 inches and is about ¼ inch thick. Cut twelve 5 by 2-inch rectangles, using a pastry wheel. Brush around the edges of each rectangle with beaten egg and then place about 1 ounce of chocolate in the center of each rectangle.

2 Fold up the rectangles lengthwise, wrapping the chocolate in the dough. Press the edges down to seal well, then brush the pastries with egg glaze. Snip through the top of the dough to make a steam vent with scissors. Place pastries about 2 inches apart on a lightly greased or parchment-lined baking sheet. Let pastries rise for 30 minutes.

3 Preheat the oven to 350°F. Bake croissants for 30 minutes or until nicely browned. Let cool on a rack, then serve.

BRIOCHE

Brioche is too rich to be considered bread, but too breadlike to be considered cake. Regardless of what category it falls into, a brioche is a lovely breakfast pastry that is easy to make. The sponge is designed to give the yeast and gluten a head start before you add the salt, eggs, and butter, which significantly inhibit the rising and structuring of brioche. If all the ingredients were mixed together at once (as in most breads), the dough would be heavy and slow to rise.

The amount of sugar in this recipe may easily be varied to reflect your particular use and preference. Brioche dough is sticky and difficult to handle, but the results are well worth it. Make a batch of small individual brioches or bake a large brioche and fill it with raisins, cinnamon, and chopped nuts. Brioche can also be filled with whipped cream, for an exciting and different pastry.

BREAKFAST BRIOCHES

**MAKES ABOUT 2½ POUNDS
DOUGH or 16 INDIVIDUAL
BRIOCHES**

INGREDIENTS

¾ cup butter
½ cup granulated sugar
1½ teaspoons salt
3 large eggs
3 cups all-purpose flour
2 large eggs, lightly beaten

BASIC SPONGE

½ cup milk
½ cup hot water
*2 packages active dry yeast
  or 1 cake (1½ ounces)
  fresh yeast*
2 cups all-purpose flour

1 First prepare the sponge. Mix the milk and water, then stir in yeast. Place flour in a mixing bowl and gradually add the liquid mixture, stirring until smooth. Cover and let rise at room temperature for about 45 minutes to 1 hour.

2 In a large bowl, cream the butter with the sugar and salt. Mix in the eggs, one at a time, then add the flour. When the mixture is smooth, add the sponge and knead the dough for about 10 minutes, or until smooth and elastic.

3 Place dough in a greased bowl, cover, and let rise at room temperature for about 1½ to 2 hours, or until doubled in bulk. Punch down and refrigerate for at least 4 hours. This chilling will allow the dough to rise more slowly, because the yeast is inhibited by temperatures near the freezing point. The chilling also gives you a dough that is easier to shape. At this point, the brioche dough can be stored in the refrigerator for up to 1½ days before it begins to deteriorate.

4 Divide the dough into 16 equal pieces. Round each piece into a ball, then "saw" back and forth with a finger to create a small "head" on each. Don't break the connection, however. Now place each shape into a well-greased brioche mold and press top "head" down onto bottom ball. Brush brioches with beaten egg and set aside to pan-proof for at least 30 minutes.

5 Preheat oven to 350°F. Place brioche molds on a baking sheet, leaving about 2 inches space between them. Bake for about 20 minutes, or until they are well browned. Let cool briefly, then remove from molds and let cool on a rack.

CINNAMON-NUT BRIOCHE LOAF

SERVES 8

INGREDIENTS

½ batch Brioche Dough
½ cup granulated sugar
1 tablespoon ground
  cinnamon
¼ cup raisins
¼ cup chopped walnuts
1 large egg, lightly beaten

1 Roll out the dough onto a work surface to form a rectangle measuring 6 by 12 inches and about ¼ inch thick. Slice the dough in half lengthwise and separate halves. Place lower half onto a lightly greased or parchment-lined baking sheet. Brush the beaten egg around the edge on all sides.

2 In a small bowl, mix the sugar with the cinnamon, raisins, and walnuts. Spread the filling along the brioche strip and then place the other half on top. Trim the edges with a pastry wheel to make a neat loaf. Use the trimming scraps to make a leaf and vine design, as shown. Glaze the top of the brioche with beaten egg, and place design on top, then glaze design as well. Let the pastry pan-proof for at least 30 minutes.

3 Preheat the oven to 350°F. Bake the brioche loaf for about 40 minutes, or until the sides are well browned. Let rest for 15 minutes, then serve warm.

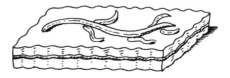

KUGELHOPF

INGREDIENTS

½ cup dark raisins
⅓ cup light raisins
¼ cup brandy, preferably
    apple, cherry, or apricot
½ cup (1 stick) butter
½ cup granulated sugar
½ teaspoon salt
3 large eggs
2 cups all-purpose flour
⅔ cup milk
½ cup sliced almonds
Confectioners sugar

SPONGE

⅓ cup milk, heated to
    105°–115°F.
1 package active dry yeast
¾ cup all-purpose flour

Kugelhopf is a type of brioche made in a traditional kugelhopf mold, similar to a Bundt pan but higher and not as wide.

1 Prepare the sponge. Place milk in a bowl, add the yeast and stir in the flour. Mix until you have a sticky dough. Cover and let rise for about 30 minutes, or until doubled in bulk.

2 Soak the raisins in the brandy until plumped, about 15 minutes. Meanwhile, cream together the butter and sugar in a large mixing bowl and then add the salt and eggs. Beat well, then stir in the flour and milk, alternately. Add the risen sponge.

3 Drain the raisins and knead them into the dough. Turn out dough onto a floured surface and continue kneading for at least 10 minutes. Set aside briefly.

4 Butter the mold and press the sliced almonds onto the sides and on bottom. Shape dough into a doughnut to fit the mold and then place dough into mold. Let rise for 30 to 40 minutes, or until the dough comes to within 1 inch of the rim.

5 Preheat the oven to 375°F. Bake kugelhopf until well browned or until a toothpick inserted in the thickest part comes out clean, about 50 minutes. Place kugelhopf upside down on the rack while still in the mold and let cool for 10 minutes. Then remove mold and return to right side up to cool completely. Dust with confectioners sugar and serve. Kugelhopf makes a nice tea-time snack with butter and preserves.

RUM BABAS

INGREDIENTS

1 cup half and half
4½ cups all-purpose flour
2 packages active dry yeast
½ cup + 2 teaspoons
  granulated sugar
2 tablespoons warm water
  (105°F.)
6 large eggs
1¼ teaspoons vanilla
  extract
⅛ teaspoon ground
  cardamom
½ cup (1 stick) butter,
  melted and cooled
1 tablespoon dried
  currants, soaked in rum
  until plump

Although the baba is Russian in origin, the addition of rum is attributed to Polish King Stanislas I. Leszcynski. The sugar syrup came later, as did the apricot glaze, which is French. This version is from Gerald Gliber.

1 Scald the half and half in a saucepan set over medium heat. Place 1 cup of the flour in the bowl of a mixer and pour in the hot half and half. Mix well and let cool. In a small bowl, mix the yeast with 2 teaspoons of sugar and the warm water. Let stand for 15 minutes.

2 Add the yeast mixture to the flour mixture and beat slowly for 1 minute, or until ingredients are blended well. Place a large, heavy mixing bowl into a larger bowl of hot water to warm the bowl for about 3 minutes. Lightly grease the inside of the bowl and turn in the flour mixture. Cover with a towel and set to rise in a warm spot (about 80°F.) for about 1½ hours, or until dough doubles in size.

3 Place the eggs and remaining sugar in the bowl of an electric mixer and beat with the balloon whisk at medium

RUM SYRUP

3 cups water
2¼ cups granulated sugar
*⅓ cup dark rum, or more
   to taste*

speed for 2 minutes, then at high speed for 3 to 4 minutes, or until batter forms a ribbon when whisk is lifted from bowl. Set machine at slow speed and exchange whisk for a paddle. Add the vanilla and cardamom, along with the butter and drained currants. Add the remaining flour and then the sponge. Beat 1 minute, then change speed to medium and beat for 5 minutes. Lower speed one notch and continue beating for 3 minutes.

4 Grease 10 small baba molds and fill halfway with the mixture. Return molds to a warm spot to rise for about 45 minutes, or until doubled in bulk and up to the tops of the molds. Cover dough while it rises; you can use tall glasses to keep the towel from touching the pastries.

5 When babas have nearly doubled, remove gently and place in a warm, draftless area (such as inside a kitchen cabinet). Preheat the oven to 375°F. When oven is hot, put in baba molds and bake for 40 to 45 minutes, or until a skewer inserted in the center comes out clean. Do not open the oven while they are baking.

6 Place molds on a rack to cool for 5 minutes, then cover with a tent of aluminum foil (this allows you to unmold the babas more easily). When babas have cooled to lukewarm, unmold onto a towel and cool for 10 minutes or more, turning every 3 or 4 minutes. Set upright to finish cooling.

7 While babas cool, prepare the syrup. Place the water and sugar in a deep saucepan and bring to a boil. Immediately remove from the heat and stir. Let cool, then add the rum.

8 Place babas on a rack in a pan and spoon the syrup over them until they have soaked up as much as they can hold. Pour off the extra and use again and again, to thoroughly soak the babas. Allow babas to sit until you are ready to serve. When serving, put on a plate and spoon a little extra syrup over. One of my favorite ways to eat these babas is along with poached fruit or a fruit compote. Whipped cream, vanilla pastry cream, and candied fruit are some of the more traditional accompaniments.

NOTE As an alternative, heat approximately ⅓ cup of apricot jam and brush it on the babas as a final service.

Babas can be wrapped tightly before adding the syrup, and they will keep nicely in the refrigerator for 1 week. They can also be frozen for up to 2 months, then thawed for 24 hours in the refrigerator.

Opposite: Napoleons (page 61).

BLACKBERRY CREAM SAVARIN

SERVES ABOUT 8

INGREDIENTS

Ingredients for one 10-inch large ring baba (see previous recipe)

2 cups milk

3¼ cups granulated sugar

6 large egg yolks

1 teaspoon salt

2 to 3 tablespoons blackberry liqueur

½ cup all-purpose flour

2 tablespoons butter

1 cup fresh blackberries, cleaned

3 cups water

1 Prepare the dough as directed in the previous recipe, following steps 1 to 3. Grease a 10-inch savarin ring and fill halfway with the mixture. Cover and let rise for about 45 minutes, or until doubled in bulk and up to the top of the ring mold.

2 Preheat the oven to 375°F. When oven is hot, put in savarin and bake for about 1 hour, or until a skewer inserted in the center comes out clean. Do not open the oven while savarin is baking.

3 Place savarin in the mold on a rack to cool for 5 minutes, then cover mold with aluminum foil and continue to cool for about 10 minutes more. Remove from pan and let cool completely.

4 Prepare the filling. Heat the milk with ½ cup of the sugar in a heavy stainless-steel or enamel pot. Whisk the sugar with the milk until it dissolves. Keep warm. Beat together the yolks and another ½ cup of sugar in a large mixing bowl, then add the salt and 1 tablespoon of the liqueur, and mix until smooth. Add the flour slowly, whisking it into the yolk mixture. Bring milk to a rolling boil, then whisk about ⅓ of it into the yolk mixture to temper it. Bring the remaining ⅔s of the milk mixture back to a boil over medium heat and whisk in the tempered yolk mixture. Don't stop whisking as it thickens, lest it lump up.

5 Place the butter in the bottom of a cool mixing bowl and have it ready for the custard. When the custard begins to boil and the flour in it is cooked, immediately pour through a sieve onto the butter in the bowl. Whisk the butter into the custard until it melts, then cover custard with plastic wrap, pressing lightly onto the surface. Chill for about 30 minutes.

6 Place the water and remaining 2¼ cups of sugar in a deep saucepan and bring to a boil. Immediately remove from the heat and stir. Let cool, then add the remaining 1 to 2 tablespoons liqueur. Place savarin on a rack in a pan and spoon the syrup over it until the cake has soaked up as much as it can hold.

7 When ready to serve, fold the blackberries into the custard and spoon the mixture into the center of the savarin. Serve at once.

NOTE   If desired, you can lighten the berry cream by folding in some whipped cream.

CRUMB-SPRINKLED BABKA

INGREDIENTS

1½ cups warm milk
(105°–115°F.)

2 packages active dry yeast
or a 1½-ounce yeast
cake

4 cups all-purpose flour,
approximately

½ cup (1 stick) butter

¾ cup granulated sugar

2 teaspoons ground
cinnamon

1 teaspoon salt

6 large egg yolks

½ cup raisins

¼ cup chopped nuts

2 tablespoons flavored
liqueur or 1 teaspoon
vanilla extract

1 large egg, lightly beaten

1 Prepare the sponge by mixing the milk, yeast, and 2 cups of flour in a bowl. Stir until well blended, then cover and let rise at room temperature for 45 minutes.

2 Meanwhile, cream the butter, sugar, cinnamon, salt, egg yolks, raisins, nuts, and flavorings in a large bowl. When the sponge has doubled in bulk, add to the creamed mixture and knead, adding as much of the remaining flour as necessary to get a smooth yet slightly sticky dough. Knead the dough for about 10 minutes, until smooth and elastic, then place in a greased bowl and cover; let dough rise for 1½ hours, or until doubled in bulk.

3 Punch dough down and shape into a large Bundt pan or 10-inch tube cake pan. Allow to rest (pan-proof) for 45 to 60 minutes at room temperature. Preheat the oven to 350°F.

CRUMB TOPPING

¼ cup granulated sugar
¼ cup (½ stick) butter
1 teaspoon vanilla extract
Scant pinch of salt
*½ to 1 cup all-purpose
   flour*

4 Meanwhile, prepare the topping. In a bowl, cream together the sugar, butter, vanilla, and salt. Add the flour gradually, rubbing it in until you have the desired crumbly texture. Glaze the top of the babka with beaten egg, and sprinkle on the crumbs. Bake for 50 to 60 minutes, or until the cake is nicely crusted and sounds hollow when tapped. Let cool for 30 minutes before serving.

DANISH PASTRIES

Danish pastries are another successful marriage between two baking concepts. They are definitely for dessert (like cake), but also layered and unfermented (like puff pastry). Also, Danish pastries should not be quite as flaky as puff pastry; they are usually turned in much the same way as croissant dough. Danish pastries contain yeast, as do the recipes in the previous chapter, however the yeast must be handled carefully and never allowed to over-ferment (rise).

More variations are possible than with puff pastry because Danish pastry is leavened by the yeast as well as by the layers of butter. However, to get the lightest possible pastry with the greatest volume, try to keep the dough thin when you fashion it into individual pastries and rings. If the butter and yeast work properly, your Danish will be delicately layered and buttery like croissants, yet light and tender as cake.

NOTE: Handle the dough as little as possible to avoid developing the gluten too much. Danish should not be as chewy as croissants. Substitute up to 25 percent cake or pastry flour for the all-purpose flour, if a "softer" dough is your desire.

Also remember that yeast doughs are best left unfrozen and that Danish dough in particular should be used as fresh as possible.

DANISH PASTRY DOUGH

MAKES ABOUT 3½ POUNDS

INGREDIENTS

*3 packages active dry yeast
  or one 2-ounce cake*
1 cup granulated sugar
1½ teaspoons salt
5 large egg yolks
*1 tablespoon vanilla
  extract*
*½ teaspoon grated orange
  rind (zest only)*
1 cup milk
4½ cups all-purpose flour
1 pound butter, very cold

Danish pastry should be flaky like croissants, and rich and sweet as a cake. It is turned (again, much like croissants) but unfermented, and used only for desserts and breakfast cakes.

1 In a large bowl, cream together the yeast, sugar, and salt. Add the yolks, one at a time, until the mixture is smooth. Then add the vanilla, orange rind, and milk. Scrape down the bowl, mix again, and add 4 cups of the flour. Mix again until smooth, about 2 or 3 minutes. Don't over-mix.

2 Cover the bowl and place dough in the refrigerator. Chill for about 1 to 1½ hours. This dough will not rise very much (seemingly not at all) because of the rich egg yolks inhibiting the essential structure of the dough, but this rest will serve not to ferment the dough but to relax the gluten strands, making it easier to handle later. Chilling the dough also makes it more compatible with the cold butter which will be incorporated later.

3 Meanwhile, soften the butter with the remaining flour, keeping the butter covered with the flour while cutting and kneading it quickly with a pastry scraper. Feel for cold lumps in the butter and break them up; add a bit more flour if necessary to soften the butter without melting it. Shape the butter into a 6-inch square.

4 Remove the chilled dough carefully and drop it onto a well-floured surface. Roll a flap from each of the 4 corners and wrap up the softened butter. Roll the dough into a rectangle about 20 inches long and 8 inches wide. Bring both ends toward the center like a book, leaving a small space in between for the spine. Fold in half, "closing" the book. Give the dough a one-quarter turn, then roll out to a rectangle and fold again. Chill for one hour, then roll out, fold, and turn again. Chill for one hour, then make one final turn and fold. After 4 turns, the dough must be refrigerated at least 3 to 4 hours before using. Remember that Danish dough is strictly for dessert. Don't handle the dough or roll it more than necessary, lest it develop too much elasticity, or chewiness.

DANISH PINWHEELS

INGREDIENTS

²/₃ batch Danish Pastry
  Dough
1½ cups raspberry,
  strawberry, or apricot
  preserves
1 large egg, lightly beaten

Different and eye-catching, these pastries take a little more effort but are well worth it.

1 Divide the dough in half and roll out one portion to form a rectangle that measures 8 by 12 inches, and is about ¼ inch thick. Trim edges, then cut into six 4-inch squares, using a pastry wheel.

2 Place about 2 tablespoons of preserves in the center of each square. Cut into each square from the corners almost to the center, using a pastry wheel. Lift, alternately, each corner and place the tip over the filling; press down. Brush pastries with beaten egg and set onto a lightly greased baking sheet about 4 inches apart. Roll out remaining dough and form in the same way. Let pastries rest at room temperature for 1 hour.

3 Preheat oven to 350°F., then bake pastries for 25 to 30 minutes, or until nicely browned and crisp. Transfer to a rack to let cool before serving.

STICKY BUNS

Photo 2 following page 100

MAKES ABOUT 1 DOZEN

INGREDIENTS

1½ cups granulated sugar
Juice of ½ small lemon
5 tablespoons water
½ cup chopped walnuts or pecans
1½ teaspoons ground cinnamon
⅓ batch Danish Pastry Dough
½ to 1 cup raisins

Also known as schnecken, or snails, these pastries have a caramelized sugar coating. Remember to handle all cooked sugar pastries with particular care.

1 Cook 1 cup of the sugar, the lemon juice, and the water in a heavy-gauge pot set over medium heat until it is amber colored. Use the caramel coating to coat the bottoms of a 12-cup muffin tin. (Note: Be very careful when handling cooked sugar. Only stir occasionally to melt the sugar and then cook all the sugar evenly. When the mixture is darkened and smooth, it will be about 350°F. Handle it carefully when coating the muffin bottoms and don't allow any of it to touch your skin, even after it looks cooler; it may still be hot enough to burn.)

2 Sprinkle a few pieces of walnut or pecan onto the cooked sugar in each muffin cup. Set the tin aside to cool while you roll out your dough.

3 Mix together the remaining ½ cup sugar and the cinnamon, then dust your counter with some of the cinnamon sugar. Roll out the dough to form a rectangle about 8 × 18

94

inches, and about ¼ inch thick. Keep tossing the sugar about, using as much as possible to dust the dough. Work the sugar into the dough with the rolling pin, then sprinkle the raisins across the dough. Roll up dough rectangle jellyroll style, as shown. Cut the log of dough into ⅝-inch-thick slices using a sharp chef's knife. You should have 12 slices. Place each slice into a muffin cup, atop the caramel coating, which will have hardened and cooled by now. Allow the buns to rise in the muffin cups in a warm place (around 90°F.), but not too near anything hot, such as a pilot light or radiator. Let rise for 1 hour, or until the dough has doubled in size.

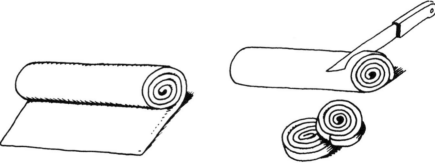

4 Preheat the oven to 350°F. Bake buns for 25 to 30 minutes, or until brown and crispy on the outside. Turn the buns out of the muffin cups immediately and leave the tin upside down on top of the buns before completely removing it. Lift off the muffin tin slowly, letting the caramel and nuts drip onto each bun. Let cool before serving.

CHEESE DANISH

Photo 3 following page 100

MAKES ABOUT 1 DOZEN

INGREDIENTS

8 ounces cream cheese
1/3 cup granulated sugar
1 large egg yolk
1 teaspoon vanilla extract
Pinch of salt
1 to 2 tablespoons grated lemon rind (zest only)
2/3 batch Danish Pastry Dough
2 large eggs, slightly beaten

This variation is a popular one with cheese, but is equally delicious with a fruit filling as well.

1 In a large bowl, mix the cream cheese and sugar until smooth and creamy but not melted. Add the egg yolk, stir, and add vanilla, salt, and lemon rind. Mix until smooth and set aside.

2 Divide dough in half and roll out one portion to form a rectangle that measures 8 by 12 inches. Trim edges, then cut into six 2-inch squares, using a pastry wheel. Take one square and pull apart 2 opposite corners to stretch the dough just a bit; this is to make the flaps for wrapping the filling. Continue by stretching the remaining squares; set aside. Roll out remaining dough and repeat, making a total of 12 squares, ready to be filled.

3 Place 1 tablespoon of cheese filling in the center of each elongated square. Brush the flaps of each with beaten egg and wrap up the filling, tucking the second flap underneath, as shown.

4 Brush entire pastry with beaten egg and place on a lightly greased baking sheet about 4 inches apart. Let rest at room temperature for 1 hour.

5 Preheat the oven to 350°F. and bake pastries for 25 to 30 minutes, or until they are browned and crispy. Let cool on a rack before serving.

ALMOND BEAR CLAWS

MAKES ABOUT 1 DOZEN

INGREDIENTS

½ cup (1 stick) butter
¼ pound almond paste
½ cup granulated sugar
2 large eggs
¼ cup all-purpose flour
⅓ batch Danish Pastry
  Dough
2 large eggs, lightly beaten

1 In a large bowl, beat together the butter and almond paste until the mixture is smooth. Add the sugar and beat the mixture until it is fluffy. Beat in the eggs, one at a time, then stir in the flour. Don't over-mix; just blend until smooth.

2 Roll out the dough to a rectangle that measures 8 by 12 inches and is about ¼ inch thick. Spread the filling across the surface thinly, up to about 1 inch from the edges. Roll the dough lengthwise to form a 12-inch-long log, then cut diagonal slices off the log in alternating directions, as shown. Separate the sections and score each at its wider edge, so as to open up the "claws" of each paw.

3 Glaze the pastries with beaten egg and place on a lightly greased or parchment-lined baking sheet about 3 inches apart. Pan-proof the pastries for 1 hour.

4 Preheat the oven to 350°F., then bake the Bear Claws for 25 to 30 minutes, or until they are nicely browned. Let cool on a rack.

DANISH CROWN LOAF

SERVES 8

INGREDIENTS

1 cup granulated sugar
1 tablespoon ground
  cinnamon
½ cup raisins
½ cup chopped walnuts
⅓ batch Danish Pastry
  Dough
1 large egg, lightly beaten

The finest use for Danish dough—simple, yet elegant.

1 Combine sugar, cinnamon, raisins, and walnuts in a small bowl and set aside.

2 Roll out dough to a rectangle 8 by 14 inches, and about ¼ inch thick. Sprinkle filling over dough, coming to within 1 inch of the edges. Roll up dough lengthwise to have a 14-inch log. Cut a horizontal notch in each end of the log, as shown. Join the ends of the log together to make an even circle and place the circle on a lightly greased baking sheet. Glaze all over with beaten egg, then cut slips about 2 inches apart all around the outside of the circle. Do not cut all the way through. Let dough rest for 1 hour.

4 Preheat the oven to 350°F., then bake the ring for at least 45 minutes, or until dough is lightly browned and crisp.

SWIRLED FRUIT POCKETS

MAKES ABOUT 1 DOZEN

INGREDIENTS

⅓ batch Danish Pastry Dough

2 large eggs, lightly beaten

¾ cup strawberry or cherry preserves, lekvar (prune puree), pureed apricots, or other filling of choice

1 Roll dough into a rectangle that measures about 10 by 16 inches and is about ¼ inch thick. Cut ¾-inch-wide strips lengthwise across the dough with a pastry wheel. You should be able to cut about 12 strips.

2 Twist each strip, rolling in 2 directions at the same time using both hands. Roll up the twisted strips snail fashion, tucking the very tail end underneath (see drawing). Press down slightly with the palm of your hand at the center of each Danish, leaving an indentation to hold the filling.

3 Brush each pastry with beaten egg around the edges, then fill each with 1 teaspoon of desired fruit filling. Place Danishes on a baking sheet about 4 inches apart and then allow them to rise on the sheet for about 45 minutes at room temperature. They should almost double in size before baking; if not risen sufficiently, they will be heavy and dense when baked.

4 Preheat the oven to 350°F. and then bake pastries for at least 45 minutes, or until they are brown and crispy at the edges. Transfer to a rack to cool.

Opposite: Swirled Fruit Pockets.
Page following: Sticky Buns (page 94).

CAKES

Opposite: Chocolate Raspberry Cake (page 108).
Page preceding: Cheese Danish (page 96).

Show a beautifully decorated cake to a small child and you will get that child's full attention almost every time. There is something about cakes (big or small) that excites people, whether they are big or small, too. The appeal is as universal as the effect. Cakes hold a hidden surprise that waits to be discovered. The spell is broken by eating through the beautiful frosting you were just before admiring.

There is an infinite variety of cakes to be made, but they can be broken down into two basic categories: sponge cakes and creamed cakes.

Sponge cakes, such as genoise, are leavened with beaten eggs. The air bubbles trapped by the warmed and beaten eggs explode in the heat of the oven, raising and lightening the batter. The eggs may be separated into yolks and whites before beating, allowing the whites to achieve a greater volume on their own before you fold them into the batter. This lighter and slightly higher cake may or may not be preferable, depending on the desired result. Sponge cakes are sometimes called souffléed cakes.

The other basic approach to cake baking is the creamed batter, such as the Whole-wheat Carrot Cake in this chapter. Here the butter is first creamed with the sugar (or honey) and then mixed carefully with the eggs and flour. The leavening is usually provided by baking soda or baking powder. Because of the presence of a chemical leavener, these cakes can be mixed with a variety of ingredients (some quite heavy) and they still rise up; they are more forgiving than sponge cakes.

Creamed cakes are moist and rich, but they cannot be sliced and rolled in the number of ways that sponge cakes can. A sponge cake can be the vehicle for many desserts, but the carrot cake (and Devil's Food Cake, too) is just fine on its own, and actually seems to get better after it is wrapped well and refrigerated for a day or two.

There are no strict rules governing the decorating of cakes. These days, anything goes. But do keep these suggestions in mind when you prepare your cakes:

• Keep frostings and fillings within a reasonable range of each other. Buttercream may make whipped cream seem a bit light and thin when used together and vice versa. However, ganache and whipped cream seem to complement each other.

• Keep it simple. Too many flavors (like too many colors) will result in no flavor at all. You will find that certain flavors enhance one another, like chocolate and vanilla, while others seem to cancel each other out. The same applies to decorating. Show off your cake by framing it. Remember that a picture frame should not dominate the work of art, but rather enhance it.

• Keep it balanced. A decorated cake should be more cake than frosting. Make each mouthful contain a delicious combination of frosting, cake, and flavoring. As a teacher of mine used to say, "put some butter on your toast," and not vice versa.

BASIC SPONGE CAKE

MAKES ONE HIGH 8-INCH LAYER or ONE 13-BY-18-INCH SHEET

INGREDIENTS

6 large eggs
1 cup granulated sugar
½ teaspoon salt
1 teaspoon vanilla extract
1 cup all-purpose flour
3 to 5 tablespoons butter, melted (see note)

A classic, this cake (genoise) is light and buttery. Sponge cake has the advantage of excellent keeping qualities. Layers may be made in advance and frozen or refrigerated. An electric mixer or egg beater is necessary, however, to achieve the proper batter consistency.

The ingredients in a sponge cake are relatively simple, and vary only slightly from one recipe to another. This is because techniques and procedures determine its quality. If proportions are varied even slightly, the cake will not rise nor will it have the proper structure. More or less butter may be added, but the proportions for eggs, sugar, and flour must remain almost constant.

1 Preheat the oven to 350°F. Lightly grease an 8-inch round cake pan with 2-inch-high sides or a standard jellyroll pan, depending on the type cake you are making.

2 Place the eggs, sugar, salt, and vanilla in a bowl set over a pan of hot water or in the top of a double boiler. Turn heat to low and whisk mixture until all the sugar is dissolved and it reaches a temperature of about 120°F. (just a bit hotter than

body temperature). Whisk steadily to ensure that none of the egg scrambles near the edges or along the bottom closest to the source of heat.

3 Begin whipping the mixture at high speed with an electric mixer or rotary egg beater for about 4 minutes, or until the batter becomes much lighter in color and increases in volume. Look for it to fall in thick ribbons from the beaters, then do not mix beyond this point. Overmixing will cause too much air to be incorporated, drying out or even collapsing the cake. Undermixing will result in a dense or even partially raw cake. If the batter falls in too thick a ribbon, the surface of the cake may be lumpy or higher at the sides than in the center.

4 Immediately begin folding in the flour, using a rubber spatula and sifting the flour directly into the bowl. Then fold in the butter, pouring it in all at once. Do not over-fold, but be certain to scrape the bottom of the bowl deliberately through and all around the batter, constantly rotating. As you mix in the flour and butter, you will notice a loss of volume; the goal at this point is to keep the loss at a minimum.

5 When the batter is mixed, pour it into the cake pan or jellyroll pan and place pan in middle of the oven to ensure even baking. Bake the round cake for 25 to 30 minutes, or until lightly browned. Bake the jellyroll for 15 to 20 minutes, or until just set. Don't let the jellyroll brown as much as a round cake. The jellyroll is thinner and will bake quicker; also, if too well done, it will be difficult to roll later on.

6 Turn the cake out of its pan within a few minutes. For a rolled cake, turn out onto a well-sugared cloth or sheet of parchment. Roll up immediately with the cloth and chill for at least 30 minutes before attempting to unroll and fill.

7 After baking, cooled sponge cakes can be wrapped well and frozen or refrigerated. Refrigerated cakes may be stored for at least a few days before slicing, filling, and decorating.

CLASSIC JELLYROLL

SERVES 6 TO 8

INGREDIENTS

1 batch Basic Sponge Cake
 batter, made without the
 butter
Granulated sugar
2 cups strawberry,
 raspberry, or other
 preserves of choice
Confectioners sugar

SYRUP (optional)

1/2 cup water
1/2 cup granulated sugar
1/4 cup liqueur to
 complement choice of
 preserves

1 Preheat the oven to 350°F. Line a standard jellyroll pan with parchment paper or grease it generously. Prepare the cake batter according to the directions in the previous recipe but omit the butter so that cake will not crack when rolled. Spread batter evenly across the pan, using a drop-level spatula if possible. Bake for only about 10 to 12 minutes, or as soon as the center of the cake is very slightly browned.

2 Remove cake from oven and run a knife around the edge to separate it from the pan. Spread a clean towel on your counter and sprinkle it with granulated sugar. Turn cake out onto the towel and remove parchment paper from bottom. Roll cake up lengthwise, with towel inside the roll. Chill or fill immediately. If desired, prepare a syrup to moisten the cake. In a saucepan, bring the water and sugar to a boil, stirring to dissolve all the sugar. Remove from the heat, then add the liqueur. Unroll cake, remove towel; brush cake with syrup.

3 Spread the preserves across the cake to within about 1 inch of the edges, and roll up again. Trim off the ends. Sift some confectioners sugar across the top and serve plain.

CHOCOLATE RASPBERRY CAKE

Photo opposite page 101

SERVES 8

INGREDIENTS

1 batch Basic Sponge Cake batter, baked in an 8-inch round cake pan

3 cups heavy cream

3 to 4 tablespoons granulated sugar

2 teaspoons vanilla extract

¼ cup unsweetened cocoa powder

½ cup raspberry preserves

1 cup fresh raspberries

SYRUP

¾ cup granulated sugar

¾ cup water

½ cup dark rum (optional)

A combination of sponge cake and whipped cream, this chocolate dessert is lighter than it looks. The chocolate and raspberry center provides a rich surprise.

1 Prepare the filling while the cake is cooling. In a bowl, whip together the cream, sugar, vanilla, and cocoa until the mixture forms firm peaks; don't overwhip.

2 Prepare the syrup. Bring the sugar and water to a boil in a saucepan set over high heat, then remove from the heat and add the rum, if desired. Set aside.

3 Prepare the ganache for the decorations. Chop the chocolate and melt together with the cream, butter, and vanilla in the top of a double boiler set over very gentle heat. Don't allow the water to boil under the chocolate. Mix gently, then remove from heat as soon as chocolate has melted.

CHOCOLATE GANACHE

2 ounces semisweet
   chocolate
3 tablespoons heavy cream
1/2 tablespoon butter
1 teaspoon vanilla extract

4 Trim and slice the cake in half horizontally. Moisten each half with some syrup, generously brushing syrup onto both sides of each layer. Set one layer on your decorating stand or a cake platter. Set other layer aside on a sheet of waxed paper.

5 Spread a thin layer of raspberry preserves across the bottom layer. Frost the layer with some of the chocolate-flavored whipped cream. Top with the second cake layer and finish off with the remaining whipped cream.

6 Dip each of the raspberries in the remaining syrup. Fit a pastry bag with a star-shaped tip and then fill bag with the remaining whipped cream. Pipe a decoration around the bottom and top of the cake, and then place the raspberries around.

7 Make a paper piping cone (see page 208) with parchment paper, fill with the ganache, and pipe a decoration on top as shown in the drawing, or run decorative lines across the top in a crisscross manner. Chill briefly before serving.

STRAWBERRY SPONGECAKE

Photo opposite page 116

SERVES 6

INGREDIENTS

*1 batch Basic Sponge Cake
batter*

*2 to 3 teaspoons ground
cinnamon*

Pinch of grated nutmeg

Pinch of ground ginger

2 pints fresh strawberries

¾ cup granulated sugar

½ cup water

*¼ cup fruit-flavored
liqueur, such as Grand
Marnier*

3 cups heavy cream

2 teaspoons vanilla extract

Although shortcake is often made with sweetened biscuit dough, this version layers strawberries and cream with a light sponge cake.

1 Preheat the oven to 350°F. Generously grease a 9-inch cake pan.

2 Prepare the cake batter according to directions on page 104, but sift in spices along with flour before mixing the batter. Continue following directions, and bake cake for 25 to 30 minutes, or until lightly browned. Remove from pan and let cool.

3 Wash and hull the strawberries, then slice in ¼-inch pieces. Set aside to dry. Bring ½ cup of the sugar and the water to a boil in a saucepan set over high heat, then remove from the heat and add the liqueur. Let cool, then macerate the strawberries in the syrup for 30 minutes. Drain and reserve syrup. Set strawberries aside.

4 Slice the cake in half horizontally and then brush both layers generously with the syrup. Place one layer on your cake-decorating stand or cake platter and put other layer aside.

5 Whip the cream with the vanilla and remaining sugar until it forms firm peaks. Spread about half of the cream on the bottom cake layer, then arrange about ⅔s of the strawberry slices on top. Place the outer ring of strawberries around the edge of the cake so that the tops of the berries extend out beyond the cake and will show through after the top layer is put on.

6 Place the other cake layer on top of the strawberry layer. Fit a pastry bag with a star-shaped tip and then fill with the remaining whipped cream. Pipe out a circle of cream on the top of the cake about 1 inch in from the edge, then arrange a row of strawberry slices inside the cream circle. Pipe the remaining whipped cream in the center and decorate center with remaining strawberries or put a single, unsliced strawberry in center.

ORANGE MOCHA CAKE

Photo 2 following page 116

SERVES 8 TO 10

INGREDIENTS

1 batch Basic Sponge Cake
batter

1 cup finely ground
hazelnuts

6 large egg yolks

1 cup granulated sugar

Zest and juice of 2 oranges
(see note)

Zest of 1 lemon

1/4 cup butter, in pieces

2 cups heavy cream

Grated semisweet chocolate
(optional)

A blend of orange, chocolate, and coffee, balanced with a light hazelnut sponge cake.

1 Preheat the oven to 325°F. Line a standard jellyroll pan with parchment paper.

2 Prepare the cake batter according to the directions on page 104, but substitute 1 cup of ground hazelnuts for 1 cup of the flour. Follow directions for preparing the batter, then pour into jellyroll pan and bake for about 15 minutes, or until just lightly browned. Let cake cool, then remove from pan.

3 While the cake cools, prepare the orange filling. In a large stainless-steel pot set over low heat, slowly whisk the egg yolks with the sugar for a couple of minutes or until the sugar melts into the eggs. Then add the orange zest and juice, the lemon zest, and the butter in pieces. Stir over low heat until the mixture thickens and starts to boil. Immediately remove from the heat and pour through a strainer. Let cool, then whip the heavy cream until stiff and fold into the orange mixture.

MOCHA BUTTERCREAM

2 ounces semisweet
  chocolate
6 large egg whites
1 cup granulated sugar
¾ cup butter, very cold, in
  pieces
1 teaspoon instant espresso
  powder dissolved in 2
  teaspoons hot water

SYRUP

½ cup water
½ cup granulated sugar
¼ cup fruit-flavored
  liqueur, such as Grand
  Marnier

4 Prepare the buttercream. Melt the chocolate in the top of a double boiler set over hot, but not boiling, water. Let cool but not harden. Whip the egg whites until they form soft peaks, then gradually add the sugar and continue to beat until whites form stiff peaks. This should take at least 10 to 15 minutes. Then add the cold butter in small amounts and whip to incorporate each until mixture is light and fluffy. The buttercream will seem to "break" or melt when the butter is first added. Just keep mixing until it comes together and whips up. Beat in the chocolate along with the instant espresso mixture.

5 Prepare the syrup for the cake. In a saucepan, bring the water and sugar to a boil, stirring to dissolve all the sugar. Remove from the heat, then add the liqueur. Set aside.

6 When the cake has cooled, cut the sponge into 4 equal pieces, lengthwise. Place the bottom layer on a decorating stand or your cake platter. Moisten with syrup, then divide the orange filling in half and spread one portion on the layer. Add a second layer of sponge cake and brush with syrup. Spread on enough mocha buttercream to equal the thickness of the orange filling below, then add third sponge layer. Brush layer with syrup, and layer with remaining orange filling. Top with last sponge layer, and brush with syrup. Spread remaining mocha buttercream on sides and top of cake, making a feathery design all around. Sprinkle top with grated chocolate or decorate with rosettes of remaining buttercream. Chill for one hour.

CHOCOLATE PEAR-MOUSSE CAKE

SERVES 10

INGREDIENTS

7 *large eggs*
1 *cup granulated sugar*
1 *teaspoon vanilla extract*
¼ *teaspoon salt*
½ *cup all-purpose flour*
½ *cup unsweetened cocoa powder*
½ *teaspoon ground cinnamon*
¼ *cup (½ stick) butter, melted*
4 *ounces white chocolate, half chopped for melting and half left whole to make shavings*

1 Preheat oven to 350°F. Lightly grease and flour two 9-inch cake pans.

2 Place the eggs, sugar, vanilla, and salt in a bowl set above a saucepan of hot water. Heat the mixture over low heat until the sugar has dissolved and eggs are warm to the touch. Whisk steadily to keep the eggs from scrambling on the sides and bottom of the bowl. When the mixture is warmed, remove from the heat and beat with an electric mixer set on high until the eggs have tripled in volume and mixture is light.

3 In another bowl, combine the flour, cocoa, and cinnamon. Place in a sifter over the beaten egg mixture and sift onto the eggs. Fold together, using a rubber spatula. When completely folded in, add the melted butter and stir gently. Turn into the prepared pans and bake for about 25 minutes, or until the cakes pull away from the sides of the pans and the centers spring back. Cool in pans for 10 minutes, then remove and cool on a rack.

PEAR MOUSSE

*1 pound very ripe fresh
  pears*
¼ cup granulated sugar
1 tablespoon lemon juice
*1½ teaspoons (½ package)
  unflavored gelatin*
3 tablespoons pear brandy
1½ cups heavy cream

SYRUP

¾ cup granulated sugar
¾ cup water

CHOCOLATE GANACHE
GLAZE

*4 ounces semisweet
  chocolate, chopped fine*
½ cup heavy cream
1 tablespoon butter

4 While cakes cool, prepare the mousse. Peel and core the pears. (If you couldn't get very ripe pears, then poach firm pears in 2 quarts of water until soft.) Puree pears in a food processor or blender, along with the sugar and lemon juice. Place the brandy in a cup and sprinkle gelatin over top to soften. Place cup into a small saucepan to serve as a hot water bath and heat brandy until gelatin has dissolved. Stir gelatin into the pear mixture and place in a bowl. Chill in refrigerator for about 15 minutes or until slightly set. Whip the cream until it forms soft peaks, then fold cream into the pear mixture. Let mousse set in refrigerator for 30 minutes before using.

5 Prepare the syrup by bringing the sugar and water to a boil in a deep saucepan. Stir to dissolve the sugar, then remove from the heat and let cool.

6 Lightly grease a 9-inch springform pan. Place one of the cake layers in the bottom, then moisten heavily with the syrup. Spread the pear mousse over the cake, making about a 2-inch layer. Place the second cake layer on top and moisten with remaining syrup. Chill the cake while you prepare the glaze.

7 Prepare the glaze. Bring the cream to a boil in a saucepan, then remove from the heat and add the chopped dark chocolate and the butter. Stir gently until all the chocolate has melted. Let cool for 10 minutes.

8 Melt the chopped white chocolate in the top of a double boiler, which has been set over hot, but not boiling, water. Let cool slightly.

9 Remove cake from refrigerator and pour the glaze over the top. Fill a paper piping cone (see page 208) with the melted white chocolate, then make 3 concentric circles on top of the glaze, about ¾ inch apart. Using the back of a knife, draw lines ½ inch apart through the white chocolate circles, starting at the center and moving the knife to the edge of the cake. This will give a wavy spider-web design. Return cake to refrigerator and chill for another hour.

10 Remove cake from refrigerator and release sides of springform pan. Shave thin pieces of chocolate from the remaining white chocolate and press them against the sides of the cake. Serve immediately, or return to refrigerator until ready to serve.

NOTE When making the pear mousse, be certain the gelatin has completely dissolved in the brandy before adding it to the mousse. If it is not dissolved, the mousse will not set properly and there will be rubbery strands of gelatin throughout. If this happens, place the pear puree over simmering water in a double boiler and stir until the gelatin strands have dissolved. Then let the mixture cool completely before folding in the whipped cream.

Opposite: Strawberry Spongecake (page 110).
Page following: Orange Mocha Cake (page 112).

HONEY SPICE CAKE

SERVES 6 TO 8

INGREDIENTS

3/4 cup (1 1/2 sticks) butter
1 1/4 cups honey
2 large eggs
1 cup milk
2 1/2 cups whole-wheat flour
1 teaspoon ground
  cinnamon
1 teaspoon ground ginger
1 teaspoon grated nutmeg
2 teaspoons baking soda
Confectioners sugar

This gingerbread, made with whole-wheat flour and honey, should be wrapped well and refrigerated after baking. The flavors will blend and improve as the days go by.

1 Preheat the oven to 350°F. Generously grease a 10-inch square baking pan with high sides.

2 In a large bowl, cream the butter with the honey. Add the eggs, one at a time, and blend well. Then add milk and mix again.

3 Sift together the flour, spices, and baking soda, then add the dry mixture to the large bowl. Blend well, but do not over-mix—stir only until smooth.

4 Pour batter into prepared pan and bake for about 40 minutes, or until the center rises back up when depressed gently with a finger. Let cake rest for about 10 minutes, then remove from pan and let cool on a rack. When ready to serve, dust top with confectioners sugar and cut into squares.

Opposite: Honey Spice Cake.
Page preceding: Chocolate Swiss Roll with
  Mocha Filling (page 118).

CHOCOLATE SWISS ROLL WITH MOCHA FILLING

Photo 3 following page 116

SERVES 8 TO 10

INGREDIENTS

12 large eggs, separated
1 cup granulated sugar
1 cup unsweetened cocoa powder, preferably Dutch-process
8 ounces semisweet chocolate
1½ cups heavy cream
2 teaspoons vanilla extract
¼ cup instant coffee powder
¼ cup coffee-flavored liqueur
Candy coffee beans (optional)

This "soufléed" chocolate cake is flourless. It is a little more difficult to handle, but results in a very moist and light cake.

1 Preheat the oven to 350°F. Generously grease a standard jellyroll pan, then line with parchment paper all around, extending the edges up past the edges of the pan.

2 Whip the egg yolks with the sugar until light, then slowly add the cocoa powder and blend until smooth.

3 Whip the egg whites just until firm, then fold into the yolk mixture. Pour batter into jellyroll pan and bake for 22 minutes; do not over-bake. (Note: the cake will rise and fall like a soufflé.)

4 Meanwhile, melt the chocolate with ¼ cup of the cream and the vanilla in the top of a double boiler set over low heat. When melted, blend and set aside.

5 Whip the remaining cream until firm, then blend in the instant coffee and flavor with the liqueur.

6 Turn the cooled cake out onto a well-sugared sheet of aluminum foil or parchment paper. Peel away the bottom parchment paper that had been lining the pan. Spread the melted chocolate glaze over the cake and let set for a few minutes.

7 Spread most of the mocha-flavored whipped cream across the chocolate glaze and then roll up the cake lengthwise, using the long side of the parchment or foil to lift and roll the cake. Place seam-side down on a cake platter and then decorate top with pipings of mocha cream diagonally across. Garnish with candy coffee beans, if desired. Chill cake for at least 1 hour before serving.

TOASTED COCONUT CAKE WITH LEMON-LIME FILLING

INGREDIENTS

1 cup vegetable shortening
2 cups granulated sugar
3½ cups cake flour
4 teaspoons baking powder
1 teaspoon salt
1 cup coconut milk
1 teaspoon vanilla extract
¼ teaspoon almond extract
8 large egg whites (about 1 cup)
3 cups heavy cream
¼ cup confectioners sugar
1 cup grated fresh coconut

1 Preheat the oven to 350°F. Generously grease and flour two 9-inch round cake pans.

2 In a large bowl, cream together the shortening and sugar. Sift together the cake flour, baking powder, and salt, then add to the creamed mixture, alternating with the coconut milk and ending with the milk. Stir in the vanilla and almond extracts.

3 Beat the egg whites until they form stiff peaks, then fold into the batter. Turn batter into the prepared cake pans and bake for about 25 minutes, or until a cake tester comes out clean when inserted in the centers. Let cakes cool in the pans for 10 minutes, then remove and let cool completely on a rack.

4 Prepare the filling. Scrape the zest from the lemons and limes, then squeeze the juice. Mince the zest pieces.

FILLING

3 ripe lemons
3 ripe limes
8 large egg yolks
1½ cups granulated sugar
½ cup (1 stick) butter, in pieces

5 In a stainless-steel pot, whisk together the egg yolks and sugar until blended. Add the zest and lemon and lime juice, then add the butter pieces. Place the pot over low heat and slowly bring mixture to a boil, whisking constantly. Let boil for 30 seconds while you continue to whisk mixture. Remove pot from the heat and pour mixture through a strainer into a cool bowl. Lay on a piece of plastic wrap to cover mixture, pressing it to the surface of the mixture. This will prevent a skin from forming. Chill for at least 1 hour, or until completely cold.

6 Whip 1 cup of the cream until it forms soft peaks, then fold into the cooled filling.

7 Split the cake layers in half horizontally, using a long serrated knife. Place 1 layer on your cake plate and cover with about ⅓ of the filling. Top with a second cake layer. Spread second layer with another ⅓ of the filling and cover with third layer. Cover with remaining filling and top with remaining layer. Return cake to refrigerator to chill briefly.

8 Meanwhile, whip the remaining 2 cups of cream with the confectioners sugar until it forms firm peaks. Toast the coconut in the broiler or oven until it is light brown and crunchy.

9 Remove cake from refrigerator and cover top and sides with whipped cream. Sprinkle the top and sides with toasted coconut and chill cake for another 15 minutes.

CHOCOLATE FUDGE CAKE

Photo opposite page 149

SERVES 8 TO 10

INGREDIENTS

¼ cup butter
*1 pound semisweet
    chocolate, in pieces*
¼ cup heavy cream
2 teaspoons vanilla extract
5 large eggs, separated
Pinch of salt
½ cup granulated sugar
¼ cup ground hazelnuts
Confectioners sugar
Sweetened cocoa powder

Very rich and very chocolatey, this cake should be decorated with nothing more than a light dusting of confectioners sugar.

1 Preheat oven to 350°F. Generously grease and flour a 9-inch cake pan with high sides.

2 Melt the butter and chocolate together in the top of a double boiler set over low heat. When melted, add the cream and vanilla, stir, and remove from the heat.

3 Beat the egg whites with salt until they form soft peaks. Gradually add the sugar and beat until whites form stiff peaks.

4 Lightly beat the egg yolks, then fold them into the beaten whites and blend until smooth, but don't over-whip.

5 Fold the butter mixture into the whites and stir gently. Add the hazelnuts and mix by hand carefully so as not to deflate the mixture. Pour batter into the prepared pan and bake for 30 to 40 minutes, or until set. Allow the cake to cool before turning out onto a plate.

6 Finish off the cake with a dusting on top of confectioners sugar. If desired, cut out a pattern from parchment paper and sift the sugar across the paper cut-out, as shown, or sift a geometric design with alternating confectioners sugar and sweetened cocoa powder.

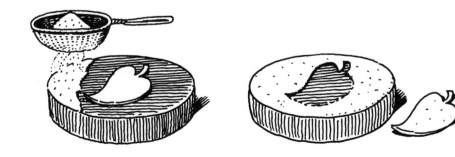

SACHER TORTE

SERVES 10

INGREDIENTS

6½ ounces semisweet
  chocolate, chopped
¼ cup (1 stick) butter
8 large eggs, separated
1½ teaspoons vanilla
  extract
¼ teaspoon salt
2 cups granulated sugar
1 cup all-purpose flour
½ cup water
¼ cup Kirsch
½ cup apricot jam

1 Preheat the oven to 350°F. Generously grease two 9-inch cake pans and line both with waxed paper. Lightly grease the waxed paper, then set pans aside.

2 Melt the chocolate and butter in the top of a double boiler set over hot, but not boiling, water. Stir to blend and let cool but do not allow to solidify.

3 Beat the egg yolks and vanilla until light and lemon colored, about 10 minutes. Add the chocolate mixture. Beat the egg whites with the salt until foamy, then begin adding 1 cup of the sugar, beating steadily until the whites form stiff peaks. Mix ⅓ of the egg whites into the chocolate mixture, then, using a rubber spatula, fold in the remaining whites and then the flour.

4 Divide the batter between the 2 pans and bake for about 45 minutes, or until the layers are puffed and dry and a toothpick inserted in the center comes out clean. Let cakes rest in the pans for 10 minutes, then remove from pans and pull off waxed paper. Let cakes cool completely on a rack.

GLAZE

4 ounces unsweetened chocolate, chopped
1 cup heavy cream
1 cup granulated sugar
1 tablespoon light corn syrup
1 teaspoon vanilla extract
1 large egg

5 While cakes are cooling, bring the remaining cup of sugar and the water to a boil. Remove from the heat and add the Kirsch. When the cakes have cooled, moisten the bottom layer with the syrup, then spread with apricot jam. Place second layer on top and moisten with remaining syrup. Place cake in refrigerator to chill while you prepare glaze.

6 Combine all ingredients for the glaze except the egg in a heavy saucepan set over low heat. Cook, stirring until the chocolate and sugar are melted, then increase heat to medium and cook for 5 minutes, or until the mixture reaches a soft ball stage on a candy thermometer (235°F.).

7 Beat the egg in a small bowl, then stir in about ¼ cup of the chocolate mixture. Add the egg mixture to the chocolate and cook, stirring briskly, for 3 or 5 minutes, or until the glaze coats the back of a spoon. Cool glaze to room temperature.

8 Holding the saucepan about 2 inches from the cake, pour the glaze evenly over the top and smooth with a metal spatula. Let glaze run down the sides of the cake. Let cake stand until glaze stops dripping, then return cake to refrigerator until glaze hardens. Remove cake from refrigerator about 20 minutes before serving.

DOBOS TORTE

SERVES ABOUT 8

INGREDIENTS

1 batch Basic Sponge Cake batter

2 ounces semisweet chocolate, chopped

1 cup granulated sugar

½ cup (1 stick) butter

3 cups confectioners sugar

1 cup chopped walnuts or almonds

½ cup heavy cream

This famous Viennese cake is usually made with paper-thin layers of sponge cake, but baking the layers can be very difficult. This version is an adaptation, far easier to achieve in the home kitchen.

1 Preheat the oven to 350°F. Lightly grease two 8-inch round cake pans. Divide the batter evenly between the pans and bake the cakes for 20 to 25 minutes, or until the centers spring back when pressed with a finger. Let cakes cool in the pans for about 10 minutes, then turn out onto a rack to cool completely.

2 Melt the chocolate in the top of a double boiler set over hot, but not boiling, water. Let cool to lukewarm; do not allow to set.

3 Cut each of the layers in half horizontally, then select the layer that has the most level top and set it aside on a piece of waxed paper. Place one of the other layers on your cake platter.

4 Melt the sugar in a heavy-bottomed saucepan and continue to cook over low heat until the sugar begins to caramelize. Watch it carefully and cook, without stirring, until it turns medium-dark brown. Pour the caramel over the cake layer on the waxed paper, spreading it neatly and evenly to the edges of the layer but not over. Let cool slightly, then cut individual wedges through the caramel topping to break it into serving slices.

5 Cream the butter with the confectioners sugar in a large bowl and beat until smooth. Stir in the lukewarm melted chocolate and blend well. Spread ⅓ of the buttercream on the bottom layer of the cake, then add another layer. Spread with another ⅓ of buttercream, then add a third layer. Spread with remaining buttercream and top with reserved caramel layer. Press the chopped nuts around the sides of the cake and then pipe rosettes of whipped cream around the bottom edge of the cake. Chill briefly, then serve.

BLACK FOREST CAKE

INGREDIENTS

1 batch Basic Sponge Cake
  batter, made with ¾ cup
  flour and ¼ cup
  unsweetened cocoa
  powder
8 ounces fresh or canned
  pitted cherries (see note)
½ cup water
½ cup + 2 tablespoons
  granulated sugar
¼ cup Kirsch
4 cups heavy cream
1 tablespoon vanilla
  extract

A favorite, well worth the effort.

1 Preheat the oven to 350°F. Lightly grease an 8-inch round cake pan with 2-inch-high sides. Pour the batter into the pan and bake the cake for 25 to 30 minutes, or until the center springs back when gently pressed with a finger. Let cake cool in the pan for 10 minutes, then remove and let cool completely on a rack.

2 Bring the water and ½ cup of the sugar to a boil in a heavy saucepan, then remove from the heat and stir in the Kirsch. Cut the cake layer in half horizontally, and place one layer on your cake platter. Moisten the layer with at least ½ cup of the syrup.

3 Whip the cream with the remaining 2 tablespoons of sugar and the vanilla until it forms firm peaks. Spread a generous layer of whipped cream over the layer and add all but one of the cherries, distributing them across the whipped cream.

4 Moisten both sides of the remaining layer with the rest of the syrup, and place it carefully onto the cherries. Using about 1 cup of whipped cream, fill a pastry bag fitted with a no. 6 star tip and set aside. Frost the sides and top of the cake with the remaining whipped cream, then pipe a circle of rosettes around the top of the cake and add one at the center. Place the remaining single cherry into the center of the center rosette and chill the cake briefly before serving.

NOTE If using fresh tart cherries or slightly under-ripe sweet cherries, macerate them for about 30 minutes in a little of the syrup before adding them to the cake.

CHOCOLATE MACADAMIA-NUT MARBLE CAKE

SERVES 8 TO 10

INGREDIENTS

1 cup (2 sticks) butter
2 cups granulated sugar
1 large egg
1 teaspoon vanilla extract
2 cups all-purpose flour
½ teaspoon salt
2 teaspoons baking powder
1 teaspoon baking soda
2 cups sour cream
8 ounces semisweet
　chocolate
1 cup shredded coconut
1 cup chopped macadamia
　nuts

This cake is rich with sour cream, chocolate, coconut, and macadamia nuts—everyone's favorite treats. Since the cake contains so many elements, keep the finishing simple, with just a dusting of confectioners sugar.

1 Preheat the oven to 350°F. Lightly grease a 10-inch tube pan.

2 Melt the chocolate over hot, but not boiling, water. Set aside to cool briefly.

3 In a large mixing bowl, cream the butter and sugar until light and fluffy. Add the egg and vanilla and mix well.

4 Sift together the flour, salt, baking powder, and baking soda. Stir half the dry mixture into the cream mixture, then add 1 cup of sour cream. Add remaining flour mixture and remaining sour cream, stirring well.

5 Remove ⅓ of the batter and place in a smaller bowl. To the remaining batter in the large bowl, fold in the chocolate. Stir in the nuts.

6 To the smaller portion of batter, add the coconut. Turn half of the chocolate batter into the cake pan, then spread the coconut batter over. Add the remaining chocolate batter and run a knife through to swirl layers. Bake cake for 1 hour, or until a tester inserted in the thickest part comes out clean.

7 Let cake cool in the pan for 10 minutes, then turn pan upside down on a rack for another 10 minutes. Remove pan and let cake cool at least 30 minutes before slicing. Sift confectioners sugar over the top and serve.

WHOLE-GRAIN CARROT CAKE

SERVES 8

INGREDIENTS

1½ cups honey
4 large eggs
½ cup butter, melted
1 teaspoon vanilla extract
1 teaspoon salt
2 to 3 tablespoons ground
   cinnamon
3 cups grated carrots
2 cups stone-ground
   whole-wheat flour
2 teaspoons baking soda

ICING

½ pound cream cheese, at
   room temperature
¼ cup (½ stick) butter, at
   room temperature
1 teaspoon vanilla extract
Zest of ½ lemon
¼ cup honey

1 Preheat the oven to 350°F. Generously grease a 10-inch Bundt pan.

2 In a large bowl, mix the honey, eggs, butter, vanilla, salt, cinnamon, and carrots. In a small bowl, sift together the flour and baking soda, then quickly add to the larger bowl and blend well, but do not over-mix. Pour batter into prepared pan and bake for 50 minutes, or until a toothpick inserted in the thickest part comes out clean. Let cake sit for about 10 minutes, then remove from pan to cool on a rack.

3 While the cake cools, prepare the icing. Cream the cream cheese with a wooden spoon or mixer paddle until soft but not melted. Add the butter and then the remaining ingredients. Mix until light and fluffy.

4 Spread the icing on the top and partly down the sides of the cake. If desired, garnish with additional lemon zest.

Opposite: Whole-Grain Carrot Cake.

PETITS FOURS GLACÉED

INGREDIENTS

12 ounces almond paste
  (about 1½ cups)
1 cup (2 sticks) butter
1 cup granulated sugar
5 large eggs
1⅓ cups all-purpose flour
½ teaspoon salt
2 ounces semisweet
  chocolate, chopped

FONDANT

3 cups granulated sugar
1 cup water
¼ cup light corn syrup

1 Preheat the oven to 350°F. Generously grease a standard jellyroll pan.

2 Cream together the almond paste, butter, sugar, and salt until mixture is smooth. Add the eggs one at a time, and beat until smooth. Add the flour all at once and mix again, but only for about 15 seconds; do not over-mix.

3 Pour the batter into the prepared pan and bake for about 15 minutes, or only until just colored lightly. Let cool for about 15 minutes.

4 Cut the cake layer in half crosswise, and spread a very thin layer of preserves on one half. Place the other half on top, with the baked top side down facing the preserves.

5 Cut out petit four shapes of diamonds, squares, rectangles, and circles. You may be able to use cookie cutters, depending on the style you have; otherwise, cut shapes out with a knife. Place individual cut-outs on a cooling rack to cool completely.

6 While the cakes cool, prepare the fondant. Bring the sugar, water, and syrup to a boil in a deep saucepan and boil until the mixture reaches 236°F. on a candy thermometer. It is best to use a heavy gauge pot with high sides and to brush down the sides of the pot with a pastry brush while the sugar cooks to keep the sugar from crystallizing on the sides.

7 When sugar reaches 236°F., remove from heat and pour into a cool stainless-steel bowl. Let cool to 115°F., then pour the fondant onto a cool, smooth work surface, preferably marble. Knead fondant with a large metal scraper or spatula until it is smooth and white, about 10 to 15 minutes. Be careful not to allow any fondant to touch your skin. Let fondant rest for at least 30 minutes before using.

8 Pour the prepared fondant over the cake shapes, covering the sides and tops. Try to cover them neatly with one application, to avoid lumps or smears. Let cool.

9 Melt the chocolate in the top of a double boiler set over hot, not boiling, water. Make a small paper cone with parchment paper (see page 208) and snip off the very tip. Let the melted chocolate cool slightly, then pour into the piping tube. Pipe out designs as desired (see photo), making swirls, spirals, scrolls, flower shapes, pinwheels, and so on. Chill until ready to serve.

BLUEBERRY POUNDCAKE WITH FRESH LEMON GLAZE

INGREDIENTS

1 cup (2 sticks) butter
1½ cups granulated sugar
3 large eggs
3 cups all-purpose flour
1½ teaspoons baking soda
½ teaspoon salt
1 pint fresh blueberries
1 cup plain yogurt
Zest and juice of 2 lemons

GLAZE

2 cups confectioners sugar
¼ cup fresh lemon juice

1 Preheat the oven to 350°F. Grease a 10-inch tube pan or Bundt pan.

2 In a large mixing bowl, cream the butter with the sugar until light and fluffy. Add the eggs one at a time, and mix well. Sift together the flour, baking soda, and salt. Add the blueberries to the flour and toss to cover fruit with flour mixture. (Flouring the fruit before adding to the batter prevents the berries from sinking to the bottom of the pan.)

3 Stir the yogurt into the butter-sugar mixture, then add the flour and blueberries. Stir in the lemon zest and juice. Turn the mixture into the pan, and bake for 50 to 60 minutes, or until a cake tester inserted in the thickest part comes out clean. Remove cake from oven and let cool for 15 minutes in the pan, then invert cake onto a rack and let cool another 15 minutes upside down. Remove pan; place right side up on rack.

4 Prepare the glaze by mixing the confectioners sugar with the lemon juice until smooth. Pour glaze over still-warm cake and let it run down the sides. Cool before serving.

DEVIL'S FOOD CAKE

SERVES 6 TO 8

INGREDIENTS

1 cup all-purpose flour
½ teaspoon baking soda
¼ teaspoon salt
¼ cup unsweetened cocoa
   powder
¼ cup (½ stick) butter
1 cup light brown sugar
1 large egg
¾ cup buttermilk
2 teaspoons vanilla extract

CHOCOLATE BUTTERCREAM

4 ounces semisweet
   chocolate
1 pound butter
½ pound confectioners
   sugar
3 large egg yolks
½ teaspoon salt
2 teaspoons vanilla extract

Dark and rich, this cake can also stand on its own or be garnished simply with a dollop of whipped cream instead of the chocolate buttercream.

1 Preheat the oven to 350°F. Generously grease an 8-inch round cake pan with high sides.

2 Sift together the flour, baking soda, salt, and cocoa powder.

3 In a large bowl, cream the butter and sugar until smooth, then beat in the egg and mix well. Add the buttermilk and vanilla, then the dry mixture all at once and beat only for a few seconds; do not over-mix.

4 Pour batter into prepared pan and bake for about 40 minutes, or until the center of the cake is set. Remove from the oven and let sit for 10 minutes, then remove from pan. Let cool completely on a rack.

5 While the cake cools, prepare the chocolate buttercream. Melt the chocolate over hot, not boiling, water, then let cool. In a large bowl, cream the butter with the confectioners sugar until blended. Add the yolks, one at a time, until mixture is smooth and fluffy. Add the melted chocolate all at once and beat until smooth again. Don't over-mix.

6 Cut the cake layer in half horizontally and place the bottom layer on a cake platter. Frost the layer with about ¼ of the buttercream, then top with the second layer and frost sides and top, reserving about ½ cup of the buttercream for the decoration.

7 Fit a pastry bag with a star-shaped tip and then fill with the remaining buttercream. Pipe *fleurettes* around the top of the cake.

NOTE The sides of the cake may be finished with chopped toasted nuts, but don't add any additional elaborations beyond that. Too many components can detract from the flavor and appearance of this cake.

CHOCOLATE SOUFFLÉ CUPCAKES

MAKES 12

INGREDIENTS

1 pound semisweet chocolate
1 cup (2 sticks) butter
1 pound confectioners sugar
8 large eggs, separated
2 teaspoons vanilla extract
½ teaspoon salt
Confectioners sugar

Light and crispy on the outside, these cupcakes are also dense chocolate richness on the inside.

1 Preheat the oven to 375°F. Line the cups of a 12-cup muffin tin with paper cupcake liners.

2 Melt the chocolate in the top of a double boiler over low heat until melted. Cool to room temperature, but do not let set.

3 Cream together the butter and confectioners sugar until fluffy and the mixture is completely white. Add the egg yolks, slowly beating them into the mixture, then add the vanilla. Fold in the cooled melted chocolate, then set aside ⅓ of the mixture.

4 Whip the egg whites and salt until they form stiff peaks, then fold in the ⅔s batch of chocolate batter. Pour mixture into the muffin cups and bake for 30 minutes, or until they are set and no longer liquid at the center. Cupcakes will rise

up and be very crispy outside and moist on the inside. Remove from oven and let cool. Cupcakes will crack slightly and fall in the centers when cooling.

5 When cupcakes are cool, sift confectioners sugar over the tops. With the remaining ⅓ chocolate mixture, fill a pastry bag fitted with a star tip and pipe a rosette into the center of each cupcake.

CREAM-FILLED CUPCAKES

MAKES 12

INGREDIENTS

*1 batch Basic Sponge Cake
batch*

3 cups heavy cream

*1½ tablespoons granulated
sugar*

2 teaspoons vanilla extract

1 Preheat the oven to 350°F. Line 12 cupcake cups with paper liners and fill each about ⅔s full with the batter. Bake for about 20 to 25 minutes, or until the surface of the cupcakes is browned and lightly crusted. Remove from oven and let cool on a rack.

2 Whip the cream with the sugar and vanilla until it forms firm peaks. Fit a pastry bag with a no. 2 plain tip and place most of the whipped cream in the bag. Pipe some cream into each cupcake from above, pushing the pastry tip through the crust and into the center of the cupcake. When the cupcake puffs up a little or feels a bit heavy, stop squeezing.

3 Fit another pastry bag with a no. 5 or no. 6 star tip and fill it with the rest of the whipped cream. Finish off each cupcake with a rosette on top, covering the hole at the center through which you piped the filling. Chill until ready to serve.

NOTE For variety, you could sprinkle chocolate shavings on top or top the cupcakes with a glaze of melted chocolate. You could also flavor the whipped cream with chocolate liqueur or use a chocolate-flavored sponge cake.

ASSORTED OTHER PASTRIES

From cheesecake to White Chocolate Mousse in Tulip Cups, these desserts do not fall into any of the specific categories discussed so far, but they belong here nonetheless.

What makes baking different and exciting is just this kind of endless combining of pastry doughs, fillings, and toppings. These desserts do just that, using pie crusts, cake batters, meringue layers, and such layered with flavored whipped cream, pastry cream, fruits, cheese, and so on. I hope this chapter will teach you that baking can be artistic, if only the pastry components are properly prepared and creatively combined and presented.

MERINGUES

Sugar and egg whites whipped together make meringue. The proportions must be two parts sugar to one part egg white, which makes for a very sweet result. If much less sugar is used, however, the meringue suffers, especially in texture. Always add a pinch of salt to the egg whites as you start to beat them to help them whip. When they do begin to whip, add the granulated sugar slowly, in several stages. If you add the sugar too quickly, it will not incorporate properly, and your meringues are likely to "weep" little translucent tears of sugar, spoiling the effect of your pastry. Over-beating is rarely a problem with meringues; impatience is more common. Add the sugar very slowly, and whip the whites five or ten minutes longer to achieve the smoothest and finest results.

Should you use a copper bowl? Egg whites can be beaten in any large bowl as long as it is grease-free (remember, grease is the enemy of egg whites). Always use a large, soft balloon whisk, which is also clean and dry. Copper bowls do react a bit with the egg whites, lending a little color and structure, however if your eggs are well-separated, the whites will whip up properly and not having a copper bowl will not make a significant difference.

A few drops of rosewater can also add a subtle variation to your meringue, however be sure to add it or any other flavoring very slowly and carefully, testing all along. One half cup of cocoa powder added to 8 egg whites and 2 cups of sugar, for example, will make a nicely flavored chocolate meringue.

MERINGUE LAYERS   Meringue batter can be piped out in a variety of ways. If you want to make individual cookies or small pastries, form the meringue into strips, ovals, or dots. To make layers for a cake, pipe the meringue into coils on a baking sheet. To bake meringues, set your oven on a low temperature, about 250°F., and bake until meringues are slightly crisp. Always store meringues in an airtight container, because humidity in the air will make them lose their crispness.

SWISS MERINGUE BUTTERCREAM   A very nice buttercream filling can be made from meringue. It is especially useful because, once made, it can be stored safely in the refrigerator for at least one week. Also, it can be warmed up and re-whipped after chilling (more than once), making it particularly practical and versatile.

To make a Swiss Meringue Buttercream, mix 8 egg whites (about 1 cup) with a pinch of salt and 2 cups of sugar in the top of a double boiler or a bowl set over hot water. Heat gently, and whisk constantly to be certain that all the granulated sugar is dissolved and that the entire mixture heats evenly. When it is hot but not overheated (about 130°F.), whip on high speed for at least ten minutes or until the whites form very stiff peaks. The egg whites and sugar are cooked as the first step in order to help structure the meringue more firmly and also because the buttercream is otherwise not cooked or baked. *Do* use an electric mixer; to attempt this whipping by hand is a laborious and frustrating experience. Any kind of electric mixer is better than trying to "stiffen" a meringue by hand.

When the whites are stiff, add 1 pound of cold butter, in pieces. Add the butter while continuing to beat at medium-high speed. At first the buttercream will seem to "break" and get much too loose. Remember that it takes time for the butter to really emulsify with the other ingredients, so let the machine go for a few more minutes and your buttercream will become light and fluffy. You could substitute vegetable shortening for the butter (up to 25 percent) if you are making the buttercream on a very hot day, or if your results are just not firm enough for your purposes. Remember that shortening has a much higher melting point than butter and will therefore help stiffen the buttercream.

You'll want to flavor the buttercream. Possible flavorings are 1 cup of melted semisweet chocolate, ½ cup unsweetened cocoa powder, 2 teaspoons of vanilla extract, or ¼ cup of desired liqueur. The flavoring should be added at the very end.

Chill buttercream in the refrigerator. When using at a latter time, whip up just a bit at a time (have patience) and place the buttercream in the top of a double boiler set over warm water if it begins to separate.

MERINGUE PETITS FOURS

MAKES ABOUT 2 DOZEN

INGREDIENTS

8 egg whites (about 1 cup)
Pinch of salt
2 cups granulated sugar
1/4 cup unsweetened cocoa
   powder
1 cup raspberry or
   strawberry preserves
4 ounces semisweet
   chocolate
1 cup chopped nuts or
   chocolate shavings

1 Preheat the oven to 250°F. Line a baking sheet with parchment paper and set aside.

2 Place the whites and salt in a large, clean bowl and whip them until they start to form soft peaks. Begin adding the sugar about 1 tablespoon at a time, beating steadily until the whites form stiff peaks. Set aside about half the mixture and then fold the cocoa powder into the other half.

3 Fit a pastry bag with a no. 4 star tip and place the white meringue in the bag. Pipe out a variety of small shapes, no larger than about 2 inches. Keep the shapes approximately the same thickness, or they will not bake at the same rate. Then fill the bag with the chocolate meringue and continue making shapes, some narrow fingers, some circles, some rosettes, and some swirls.

4 Bake the meringues for about 45 minutes, or until they are slightly crisp on the outside. Set aside to cool.

5 Sandwich together the shapes that match by spreading one half with preserves. Melt the chocolate over hot, but not boiling, water and then dip some of the other meringue shapes in and then roll in chopped nuts or chocolate shavings. Place on a rack to set, then serve.

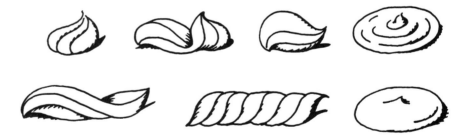

ALMOND DACQUOISE

SERVES 8

INGREDIENTS

10 large egg whites
¼ teaspoon salt
2 cups granulated sugar
1 cup ground almonds
1 cup slivered almonds,
  toasted
2 tablespoons all-purpose
  flour
Fresh raspberries (optional)

LEMON BUTTERCREAM

6 large egg yolks
2½ cups granulated sugar
3 tablespoons cornstarch
1½ cups milk, heated
1½ pounds butter, at room
  temperature
Zest of 1 lemon
Juice of 3 lemons

1 Preheat oven to 250°F. Line a baking sheet with parchment paper and trace 3 circles with the bottom of an 8-inch cake pan.

2 Whip the egg whites and salt until they form soft peaks. Start adding half the sugar about 1 tablespoon at a time, beating until the egg whites form stiff peaks.

3 Mix together the remaining sugar, the almonds, and the flour. Fold mixture into the egg whites until incorporated.

4 Fit a pastry bag with a no. 5 plain tip, and fill bag with meringue. Pipe mixture on top of the circles on the baking sheet. Begin at the center and make a disk, spiraling outward, like a snail. Bake meringue layers for 1 hour, or until they are slightly crisp on the outside. Set aside to cool.

5 Prepare the buttercream. Mix the egg yolks with the sugar in a stainless-steel saucepan. Whisk in the cornstarch. Add the hot milk to the egg mixture, pouring it in in a slow and steady stream while stirring constantly.

Opposite: Almond Dacquoise.

RASPBERRY SAUCE

*1½ cups thawed frozen
  raspberries*

*2 tablespoons framboise or
  Kirsch*

1 tablespoon lemon juice

*1 tablespoon superfine
  sugar*

6 Place the saucepan over low heat and cook, stirring constantly, until the custard thickens. Strain the custard into a bowl (don't use aluminum bowls or utensils, or they will discolor the custard) and beat until custard is at room temperature. Beat in the butter, about 3 tablespoons at a time, then add the zest and lemon juice, and beat mixture until fluffy. If the buttercream breaks or curdles, place the bowl over simmering water and heat gently until the buttercream begins to melt on the side of the bowl. Remove from heat and beat until smooth and fluffy.

7 Prepare the sauce. Place the raspberries, liqueur, lemon juice, and sugar in a blender or food processor and puree. Strain and set aside.

8 To assemble the cake, place 1 meringue layer on your cake platter or decorating stand. If necessary, trim the sides to form an even circle. Spread on a layer of lemon buttercream the same thickness as the meringue layer. Place another meringue layer on top of the buttercream, then spread on another layer of buttercream. Top with the remaining meringue layer and spread with remaining buttercream, covering sides as well as top.

9 Press the toasted almond slivers around the sides, then serve cake with raspberry sauce and fresh raspberries, if desired.

*Opposite: Chocolate Fudge Cake (page
122).*

STRAWBERRY VACHERIN

INGREDIENTS

8 egg whites (about 1 cup)
Pinch of salt
2 cups + 1 tablespoon
    granulated sugar
2 cups heavy cream
1 teaspoon vanilla extract
1 pint fresh strawberries,
    washed and hulled
½ cup apricot preserves
1 tablespoon water

Whereas the Dacquoise is a layered meringue cake, the Vacherin is a meringue crown, oftentimes filled with Swiss Meringue Buttercream (see page 144), but here it is with whipped cream and glazed fresh strawberries.

1 Preheat the oven to 225°F. Line a large baking sheet with parchment paper and trace a 12-inch circle with the bottom of a cake pan or serving dish.

2 Whip the egg whites and salt until they form soft peaks. Start adding 2 cups of the sugar, about 1 tablespoon at a time, beating until the whites form stiff peaks.

3 Fit a pastry bag with a no. 6 star tip and fill bag with meringue. Pipe a spiral to fill the 12-inch outline on the parchment paper, starting at the center and circling outward. Then pipe a series of rosettes around the edge of the circle to form a border.

4 Bake meringue for about 40 minutes, or until the meringue is very lightly crusted but not browned at all. Let cool on the baking sheet for at least 1 hour before attempting to lift it off.

5 When you are ready to fill the meringue, whip the cream until it forms soft peaks. Add the tablespoon of sugar and the vanilla, and whip until stiff.

6 Place the meringue on your cake platter and spoon a thin layer of whipped cream into the center. Arrange the strawberries on top, with their points upward in a circle, following the design of the pastry.

7 Melt the apricot preserves with the water in a small saucepan over low heat and then brush the glaze onto the strawberries. Serve as soon as possible, preferably within a few hours.

STRUDEL AND PHYLLO DOUGHS

Although they come from different countries, these two doughs are quite similar. Strudel dough is Hungarian, and it is used most often to make cheese- and fruit-filled rolls of pastry. Phyllo dough is from Greece, where the dough is cut into sheets and, when used for desserts, is layered with nuts and spices or custard. Sheets of phyllo dough are widely available in supermarkets and gourmet shops, and although you could use it to make a small strudel, if you want the real thing, you have to make your strudel dough from scratch.

Here I've included a recipe for strudel dough, plus some recipes for fillings, followed by recipes that use commercially prepared phyllo dough sheets. The strudel dough is a simple and straight-forward recipe that can be varied to taste.

BASIC STRUDEL DOUGH

INGREDIENTS

½ cup water
½ teaspoon salt
2 large eggs
1½ cups all-purpose flour,
    approximately
3 tablespoons butter,
    melted
1 cup bread crumbs

1 In a large bowl, mix the water, salt, and eggs until blended. Add the flour gradually, kneading all the while. Keep adding enough flour until you have a smooth, shiny, and elastic dough. The dough should not be sticky. Cover bowl and let dough rest for about 45 minutes to 1 hour in a warm place.

2 After the dough has relaxed, turn it out onto a card table covered with a tablecloth, and begin stretching it gently. Stretch to at least a 36-inch square, almost paper thin. Use your fingers and fists (without tearing the dough) to slowly and carefully stretch the dough across the table until it is almost transparent. If you've watched pizza makers stretch their dough, you'll understand how to use your hands to make it thinner. If your work surface is too small, allow the dough to hang over the edges. Cut off the thick edges before continuing.

3 Now brush the strudel dough all over with the melted butter and sprinkle with the bread crumbs to absorb excess moisture. The dough is ready to be filled.

APPLE STRUDEL

INGREDIENTS

½ cup (1 stick) butter
3 crisp apples
½ cup ground walnuts
½ cup raisins
1 teaspoon salt
*1 tablespoon ground
  cinnamon*
Pinch of grated nutmeg
1 cup granulated sugar
2 teaspoons vanilla extract
*1 batch Basic Strudel
  Dough*

1 Preheat the oven to 350°F. Lightly grease a very large baking sheet and and set aside.

2 In a small saucepan, melt the butter, then set aside. Peel, core, and dice the apples, then combine with the walnuts, raisins, salt, spices, and sugar in a bowl. Add the vanilla and stir to coat apples well with the spicy sugar mixture.

3 Brush the strudel dough with melted butter, then place the filling along one side to within 1 inch of the edge. Brush the side edges with melted butter and fold them toward the center to seal the ends of the pastry. Roll up the pastry, jellyroll style, using the cloth to lift the dough and roll it up and around the filling. Brush the long pastry with melted butter, then transfer to the baking sheet.

4 Bake pastry for at least 1 hour, brushing occasionally with more melted butter as it bakes. Remove from oven and let cool for about 1 hour before serving.

CHEESE STRUDEL

INGREDIENTS

¾ cup (1½ sticks) butter

8 ounces cream cheese

1 cup confectioners sugar

1 teaspoon salt

*2 teaspoons grated lemon
rind*

1 teaspoon vanilla extract

1 large egg

*1 batch Basic Strudel
Dough*

1 Preheat the oven to 350°F. Lightly grease a very large baking sheet and set aside.

2 In a small saucepan, melt ½ cup (1 stick) of the butter, then set aside.

3 Cream the cheese with the remaining butter and the sugar in a large bowl. Then mix in the salt, lemon rind, vanilla, and egg. Mix well, or until fluffy and smooth.

4 Brush the dough with some of the melted butter, then spread the filling along one side of the dough. Brush the side edges with more melted butter and fold them toward the center to seal the ends of the pastry. Roll up the dough, jellyroll style, using the cloth to lift the dough and roll it up and around the filling. Brush the edge with butter and place, seam-side down on the baking sheet. Brush the pastry with melted butter.

5 Bake the strudel for about 1 hour, or until crisp and lightly browned. Brush top occasionally with melted butter. Let cool for about 1 hour before serving.

CHOCLAVA

INGREDIENTS

*1 pound phyllo dough,
    thawed if frozen*

*3 cups shelled walnuts or
    almonds*

*6 ounces semisweet
    chocolate*

*2 teaspoons ground
    cinnamon*

Dash of ground cloves

1½ cups (3 sticks) butter

SYRUP

2 cups granulated sugar

1 cup honey

1 cup water

Rind of 1 lemon

½ cup orange liqueur

1 Preheat the oven to 375°F. Generously butter a 13 by 9 by 2-inch baking pan.

2 Place the nuts in a food processor or blender and chop finely. Watch carefully that you have chopped nuts, and do not grind to a paste. Finely chop the chocolate, then place the nuts, chocolate, cinnamon, and cloves in a bowl. Toss well, then set aside.

3 Cut the phyllo sheets to fit your pan. Reserve the cuttings. Cover the stack of leaves with a dampened towel to prevent them from drying out. Melt the butter.

4 Lay 2 sheets of dough in your pan and brush with butter. Repeat 3 or 4 more times, until you have 8 or 10 sheets. Then spread on a layer of nut mixture, about ¼ of the total. Follow with 2 sheets of phyllo, butter, and 2 more sheets. Repeat another layer of nuts, then the phyllo, again 4 sheets with butter between the 2 pairs of sheets. Repeat nuts and phyllo layers 2 more times until you have used up the nut mixture. You can use the reserved scraps between the middle layers. Top layer should again be 8 or 10 whole sheets of phyllo, with butter brushed on after every second sheet and on the top sheet.

5 With a brush or knife, push the edges of the phyllo down the sides of the pan so that you don't have ragged top edges. Now cut the pastry into serving pieces, using a sharp knife to cut all the way through, including the bottom layer. The traditional shape is diamonds, using parallel lines about 1½ inches apart. Mist the top layer with water and again 30 minutes later in the oven.

6 Place the pastry in the oven and bake for 1 hour, or until golden brown. Remove and allow to cool slightly.

7 Prepare the syrup. Place the sugar, honey, water, and lemon rind in a saucepan, and bring to a boil. Stir to blend and dissolve the sugar, reduce the heat, and simmer for 10 minutes. Remove from heat and discard the lemon rind. Allow to cool somewhat, then add the liqueur and stir.

8 Pour the warm syrup over the pastry, slowly and evenly so as pastry cools, syrup will be absorbed. Allow pastry to cool completely; in fact, it is better if allowed to rest overnight. Keep at room temperature, covered, until ready to serve.

PHYLLO ALMOND FINGERS

INGREDIENTS

¼ cup rice flour

2 tablespoons granulated sugar

2½ cups milk

½ cup heavy cream

½ cup ground almonds

1 large egg white, lightly beaten

½ cup sliced blanched almonds

½ pound phyllo sheets, thawed if frozen

½ cup (1 stick) butter, melted

If using frozen dough, allow it to thaw overnight in the refrigerator before using.

1 Prepare the syrup first. Place the sugar, water, and lemon juice in a saucepan set over moderate heat. Simmer until thickened, then stir in the orange blossom water and cook for 2 minutes longer. Let cool and then chill in refrigerator.

2 Mix together the rice flour, sugar, and ½ cup of the milk and stir to form a smooth paste. In a large saucepan, bring the rest of the milk to a boil, and then slowly add it to the paste, stirring to blend well. Pour the mixture back into the saucepan and bring to a simmer over low heat. Cook, stirring constantly until very thick. Cool completely, then add the cream and the ground almonds.

3 Preheat the oven to 350°F. Lightly grease a large baking sheet. Cut the sheets of phyllo into approximately 5 by 10-inch rectangles. Brush the center of each rectangle with melted butter.

SYRUP

1¼ cups granulated sugar
½ cup water
1 tablespoon lemon juice
*1 tablespoon orange
    blossom water*

4 Place one teaspoon of filling at one end of each rectangle. Fold the longer side slightly over the filling and roll up into a cigar shape. Place on baking sheet, leaving about 2 inches between the pastries. Brush with beaten egg white and sprinkle with sliced almonds. Bake for 20 minutes or until slightly browned. Remove pastries to a dish and cover with the chilled syrup. Let cool, then serve cold.

PASTRY DESSERTS

The recipes that follow are a varied selection of pastries and desserts, some of which combine basic doughs and batters described earlier in the book with rich fillings or custard, mousse, cream cheese, and so on. Though most pastries are assemblages of doughs, fillings, and toppings, these are classic preparations and I've grouped them together because they are just a bit special.

BOSTON CREAM PIE

INGREDIENTS

*1 batch Basic Sponge Cake
    batter (page 104)*
1 cup milk
½ cup granulated sugar
3 large egg yolks
Pinch of salt
2 teaspoons vanilla extract
¼ cup all-purpose flour
2 tablespoons butter
1⅓ cups heavy cream
*4 ounces semisweet
    chocolate*

Early versions of this American pastry did not have the chocolate topping, which we expect now. The glaze was added by Boston's famous Parker House Hotel, and it makes this a truly delicious dessert.

1 Preheat the oven to 350°F. Lightly grease an 8-inch round cake pan with 2-inch-high sides. Pour batter into cake pan and bake for 25 to 30 minutes, or until lightly browned. Let cake cool for 10 minutes, then turn out onto a rack to cool completely.

2 In a large stainless-steel pot set over low heat, bring the milk and half the sugar to a boil. Whisk together the yolks, salt, and 1 teaspoon vanilla, then slowly whisk in the flour. Beat a little of the boiling milk into this paste to temper it, then pour the tempered paste into the milk, whisking constantly. When the custard returns to a boil, let it simmer for at least 30 seconds to 1 minute, so as to cook the flour. Place 1 tablespoon of butter into the bottom of a bowl and pour the custard through a strainer into the bowl. Whisk to melt the butter into the custard,

then cover custard with plastic wrap, pressing the wrap down onto the custard surface; this keeps a skin from forming. Chill for about 30 minutes.

3 Whip 1 cup of the cream with the remaining tablespoon of vanilla and then fold into the custard.

4 Cut the cake in half horizontally and place the bottom layer on your cake platter. Spread ¾s of the custard filling on top and then place the other layer on top of the custard. Spread the remaining custard over the top and chill cake.

5 Place the chocolate, remaining cream, and remaining butter in a heavy-bottomed saucepan and cook over medium heat until the chocolate has melted. Stir gently. Add the remaining vanilla and let mixture cool to lukewarm. Spread glaze over the top and down the sides of the cake, then chill again to set the chocolate. Serve cool or at room temperature.

CHOCOLATE BAKED ALASKA

INGREDIENTS

*1 batch Basic Sponge Cake
    batter, made with ¾ cup
    flour and ¼ cup
    unsweetened cocoa
    powder (page 104)*

1¾ cups granulated sugar

½ cup water

¼ cup dark rum

*1 quart vanilla or
    chocolate chip ice cream*

*6 large egg whites (about
    ½ cup)*

Pinch of salt

1 Preheat the oven to 350°F. Lightly grease a 9-inch square baking pan with high sides. Pour the batter into the pan and spread to fill corners. Bake for 25 to 30 minutes, or until the center springs back when touched with a finger. Let cool for a few minutes, then turn out onto a rack to cool completely.

2 Bring ½ cup of the sugar and the water to a boil in a saucepan set over high heat. Remove from heat and add the rum, then let cool briefly.

3 Trim and slice the cake in half horizontally. Moisten each half with some syrup, generously brushing syrup onto both sides of each layer. Set one layer on your decorating stand or cake platter. Set other layer aside.

4 Set the ice cream out to soften for about 15 minutes, then spread half onto the bottom layer up to within 1 inch of the edge. Place second layer on top of the ice cream and top with remaining ice cream, again to about ½ inch of the edge. Place cake in the freezer to set the ice cream, about 2 hours.

5 Beat the egg whites and salt until they form soft peaks, then gradually add the remaining sugar, one tablespoon at a time, until they form stiff peaks. Spread the meringue on the sides and over the top of the cake, completely enclosing the ice cream and cake layers in the meringue. Place cake at least 5 inches from the heat of your broiler, and brown the meringue just a bit. Watch the meringue; it shouldn't brown too dark. Serve immediately.

Opposite: Chocolate Puff (page 66).

RIGÓ JANESI

SERVES 12

INGREDIENTS

3/4 cup all-purpose flour
1/2 teaspoon baking powder
1/2 teaspoon baking soda
1/4 teaspoon salt
1/4 cup ground almonds
1/3 cup unsweetened cocoa
powder
1/2 cup (1 stick) butter
1/3 cup granulated sugar
1 large egg
1 cup chocolate shavings
Whipped cream (optional)
Candied violets (optional)

This is a rich chocolate cream dessert from Vienna, with a chocolate-almond cookie crust, a chocolate cream filling, a light chocolate cake top, and a chocolate glaze.

1 Preheat oven to 350°F. Lightly grease a 9-inch cake pan and line with waxed paper.

2 Sift together the flour, baking powder, soda, and salt. Stir in the ground nuts and cocoa and blend well. Set aside.

3 Cream the butter and sugar until light and smooth. Mix in the egg completely. Mix the dry ingredients by hand into the butter mixture until ingredients are uniformly moistened. Press the dough evenly into the bottom of the cake pan and bake for about 25 minutes, or until center springs back when pressed with a finger. Let cool for 5 minutes in the pan, then remove from pan to cool completely.

4 Prepare the cake top. Keep the oven set at 350°F. Wash and dry the 9-inch cake pan, then grease and dust with flour.

Opposite: Rugelach (page 190).

CAKE TOP

3 large eggs
½ cup granulated sugar
1 teaspoon vanilla extract
¼ cup all-purpose flour
¼ cup unsweetened cocoa
  powder
1 tablespoon butter, melted

CHOCOLATE CREAM FILLING

1 cup heavy cream
8 ounces semisweet
  chocolate
¼ cup dark rum
1 teaspoon vanilla extract

CHOCOLATE GLAZE

1 cup granulated sugar
½ cup water
8 ounces semisweet
  chocolate

5 Beat together the eggs, sugar, and vanilla until tripled in volume and the batter falls from the beater in ribbons. Sift the flour and cocoa into the batter and fold to incorporate. Then fold in the melted butter and pour into prepared pan. Bake for 15 minutes, or until the cake pulls from the sides of the pan and the top springs back when pressed. Let cool for 10 minutes, then remove from pan to cool completely on a rack.

6 Prepare the cream filling. Bring the heavy cream to a boil in a saucepan. While the cream heats, chop the chocolate into fine pieces. When cream begins to boil, remove pan from the heat and add the chocolate all at once. Stir mixture until chocolate has melted, then pour mixture into a bowl and chill for 1 hour or until completely cold. Add the rum and vanilla and beat with a wire whisk until filling forms soft peaks. Be careful not to over-beat.

7 Assemble the cake. Place the cookie crust in the bottom of a lightly buttered springform pan. Put in the filling and smooth it to the edges of the pan. Place the cake layer on top of the filling. Chill in refrigerator at least 1 hour.

8 While cake chills, prepare the glaze. Bring water and sugar to a boil in a saucepan set over medium heat. While the water comes to a boil, chop the chocolate finely. When sugar mixture boils, remove from the heat and add the chocolate, stirring constantly until chocolate is dissolved. Let glaze cool 20 minutes, or until it reaches room temperature.

9 When cake is chilled and glaze has cooled down, pour on glaze and return cake to refrigerator to chill for an additional 20 minutes. When glaze has set, unmold cake from pan by running a spatula around the sides and then unsnapping form.

10 Spread the sides of the cake with the shaved chocolate. Serve cake cold, cutting each portion with a serrated bread knife and using a light sawing motion to cut through the crust. If desired, pipe rosettes of whipped cream and top with candied violets.

GATEAU ST. HONORÉ

SERVES 8 TO 10

INGREDIENTS

½ batch Flaky Pie Crust dough (page 19)

1 batch Cream Puff Batter (page 5)

2 cups milk

1¾ cups granulated sugar

6 large egg yolks

Pinch of salt

1½ teaspoons vanilla extract

⅓ cup all-purpose flour

2 tablespoons butter

Juice of ½ lemon

1 pint fresh strawberries, cleaned and hulled

½ cup apricot preserves

1 tablespoon liqueur or brandy

1 Roll out dough to fill a 9-inch circle and place circle on a baking sheet. Chill for at least 30 minutes. Preheat the oven to 350°F.

2 Lightly grease another baking sheet and place the cream puff batter into a large pastry bag fitted with a no. 8 plain tip. Pipe out 12 plain cream puffs onto the baking sheet. Bake the cream puffs for about 25 minutes, or until crusty and brown. Set aside to cool.

3 Bake the pie crust for 20 minutes, or until golden brown. Set aside. (Depending on the size of your oven, you might be able to bake the cream puffs and pie crust at the same time.)

4 Prepare the cream filling. Heat the milk with about ½ cup of the sugar in a heavy stainless-steel or enamel pot. Whisk the sugar with the milk until it dissolves. Keep warm. Beat together the yolks and ¼ cup sugar in a large mixing bowl, then add the salt and vanilla, and mix until smooth. Add the flour slowly, whisking it into the yolk mixture.

5 Bring the milk to a rolling boil, then whisk about ⅓ of it into the yolk mixture to temper it. Bring the remaining ⅔s of the milk mixture back to a rolling boil over medium heat and whisk in the tempered yolk mixture. Don't stop whisking, or the custard will form lumps. Place the butter in the bottom of a cool mixing bowl and have it ready for the custard. When the custard begins to boil and the flour in it is cooked, immediately pour through a sieve onto the butter. Whisk the butter until melted, then cover custard with plastic wrap, pressing lightly onto the surface. Chill for about 30 minutes.

6 Place the remaining 1 cup sugar in a heavy-bottomed saucepan with the lemon juice. Cook over low heat until sugar and lemon juice turns golden brown and becomes viscous.

7 Place the pie crust on your serving platter. Fill the cream puffs with the pastry cream to make a circle around the edge of the crust. Dip each cream puff into the caramelized sugar and place it, caramelized side down, around the edge of the crust. The caramelized sugar will make the cream puffs adhere to the crust, but be very careful not to get any hot sugar onto your skin. (If the caramelized sugar begins to harden, gently warm it up again, mixing carefully until it melts. Don't try to use the caramelized sugar unless it is the proper consistency.)

8 Spread a thin layer of pastry cream across the pie crust, inside the circle of puffs. Slice the strawberries and arrange them on top of the cream.

9 Melt the apricot preserves in a small saucepan with the liqueur, then strain and use as a glaze to coat the strawberries.

10 Heat the caramelized sugar again if it has hardened, so you can place the finishing touch on your *gateau.* Using a wooden spoon, "pull" the caramelized sugar in a circular motion around the edge of the pastry on top of the cream puffs but not over the berries and custard. If the sugar is just barely melted but not too loose, you will get long strands or "angel hairs." Keep teasing out the strands and pulling around and around, creating a "nest" effect. Unwanted clumps and thick pieces of sugar can be easily removed after cooling and before serving. Chill well before serving.

APPLE CHARLOTTE

SERVES ABOUT 8

INGREDIENTS

½ pound (2 sticks) butter

8 large apples, preferably
  tart

Juice of 1 lemon

1 cup granulated sugar

1 tablespoon ground
  cinnamon

¼ teaspoon grated nutmeg

½ cup raisins (optional)

1½ pounds sliced
  good-quality white bread

Confectioners sugar

Whipped cream or crème
  fraîche

1 Preheat the oven to 350°F. Set out a 1-quart soufflé or charlotte mold. Melt half the butter and set aside.

2 Slice, peel, and core the apples, then place in a large saucepan along with the remaining butter, the lemon juice, sugar, and spices. Cook over medium-low heat for a few minutes, or until soft but not mushy. Add the raisins, if using, and let cool briefly.

3 Cut the bread slices into triangles and brush one side of each liberally with melted butter. Press the triangles, buttered side out, onto the sides and bottom of the soufflé dish. Fill the mold with the apple filling. Brush the remaining bread triangles with melted butter and use to cover the top of the charlotte.

4 Place the charlotte in the oven and bake for about 20 to 25 minutes, or until the surface is golden brown. Let charlotte cool for 15 minutes, then place an inverted plate over the top and turn the charlotte over onto the plate. Dust top with confectioners sugar and serve warm, with whipped cream or crème fraîche.

ITALIAN TRIFLE

SERVES 8

INGREDIENTS

*1 pint strawberries, hulled
and sliced*

*2 to 3 tablespoons
superfine sugar*

3 tablespoons Marsala wine

3 ripe bananas

Juice of ½ large lemon

*6 kiwifruit, peeled and
sliced*

*1 Basic Sponge Cake, 8 or
9 inches round*

ZABAGLIONE CREAM

5 large egg yolks

¼ cup granulated sugar

¼ cup Marsala wine

1 cup heavy cream

This recipe is a favorite from one of my colleagues at the New York Restaurant School, Arlene Battifarano.

1 First prepare the cream. Combine the egg yolks and sugar in a large mixing bowl that can rest snugly over a slightly larger saucepan. Add about 2 inches of water to the pan and bring water to a boil, then reduce to a simmer. Beat the yolks vigorously with a wire whisk until light and fluffy, then place mixing bowl on the saucepan and continue beating until the mixture is very thick and pale yellow, about 10 minutes.

2 Remove bowl from the heat and stir in the wine. Return bowl to saucepan and continue beating until sauce thickens again. Remove from the heat and then chill well, about 30 minutes to 1 hour.

3 Beat the cream until it is almost but not quite stiff. Fold the cream into the chilled zabaglione and return to the refrigerator.

4 In a large mixing bowl, toss the berries with the sugar and Marsala, then let macerate for about 1 hour.

5 Slice the bananas about ⅓ inch thick and toss in a bowl with the lemon juice. Set aside 2 of the kiwifruit for a garnish.

6 Slice the cake into ¾-inch-wide sticks. Arrange about ⅓ of the cake sticks in the bottom of a large glass serving bowl. Drizzle over some of the syrup from the strawberries, then make a layer of strawberries, bananas, and kiwifruit in the bowl, using about ⅓ of the fruit. Pour in about ⅓ of the zabaglione cream, and repeat the layering 2 more times, ending with the zabaglione. Smooth the layer of cream and garnish with the reserved kiwi slices. Chill until ready to serve.

CHARLOTTE ROYALE

INGREDIENTS

9 large egg yolks
⅔ cup granulated sugar
5 large egg whites
⅓ cup granulated sugar
⅔ cup all-purpose flour
¼ teaspoon salt
½ cup red currant jelly
⅓ cup apricot preserves, heated and strained
1 cup fresh raspberries

FILLING

3 cups heavy cream
⅓ cup + 1 tablespoon granulated sugar
2 teaspoons unflavored gelatin
½ cup framboise

1 Preheat the oven to 425°F. Grease a 10 by 16-inch sheet pan and a 9-inch round cake pan, then line the pans (including the sides) with waxed paper or parchment paper. Grease the pans again, and lightly dust them with flour. Set aside.

2 Combine the yolks and sugar in the bowl of an electric mixer, and with the whisk attachment, beat the mixture until it is thick and lightened, and until the mixture becomes pale in color, about 5 minutes. Transfer to mixing bowl.

3 Clean and dry the whisk of the mixer, then beat the egg whites until they form soft peaks. Add the sugar and beat for about 30 seconds longer, or until the whites are stiff.

4 Alternately, fold the flour, salt, and egg whites into the yolk mixture. Spread the batter evenly in the 2 pans, and bake for about 10 minutes, or until the bottom of the cake is lightly browned. Turn the cakes out onto a lightly sugared piece of waxed paper and spread the rectangular cake with a very thin coating of currant jelly. Immediately roll the rectangular cake lengthwise into a tight jellyroll. Rewrap the cake in the original waxed paper (the paper used to line the pan), and chill for 30 minutes. Set the round cake aside.

5 While the cake is cooling, prepare the filling. Whip the cream with the ⅓ cup sugar until it is stiff. Cover with plastic wrap and refrigerate. Soak the gelatin and remaining tablespoon sugar in ¼ cup of the liqueur until softened.

6 With a thin-bladed knife, slice the jellyroll into ¼-inch slices; discard the first slice. Lightly butter a 3-quart mixing bowl and line with the slices, starting at the bottom center and working up to the rim of the bowl.

7 Heat the gelatin-framboise mixture in a small skillet, stirring constantly, until dissolved, taking care not to ignite the alcohol in the framboise. Transfer the mixture to a bowl, whisk the mixture briefly to cool it slightly, then fold the whipped cream and the raspberries gently into the gelatin.

8 Pour the whipped cream mixture into the cake-lined bowl and pack down gently. Moisten the round cake layer with remaining framboise and place on top of filling. Chill thoroughly, about 3 to 4 hours.

9 Unmold the cake onto a serving platter and brush with the glaze. Decorate the charlotte with whipped cream and fresh raspberries.

WHITE CHOCOLATE MOUSSE IN TULIP CUPS

MAKES 8

INGREDIENTS

½ cup (1 stick) butter
¼ teaspoon salt
⅓ cup granulated sugar
3 large egg whites
½ cup all-purpose flour
1 teaspoon vanilla extract
1 cup chopped green
    pistachio nuts

MOUSSE

3 egg yolks
¼ cup granulated sugar
2 tablespoons cornstarch
1 cup milk
½ pound white chocolate,
    chopped fine
2 cups heavy cream

These delicate cookie cups are filled with a light white chocolate mousse, then served with a tart plum sauce.

1 Preheat the oven to 375°F. Butter and flour 2 baking sheets, then with your finger, draw eight 5-inch circles in the flour.

2 In a large mixing bowl, cream together the butter, salt, and sugar until light and fluffy. Add whites slowly, then stir in the flour and vanilla.

3 Spread a very thin layer of batter (about 2 tablespoons) onto each circle, staying inside of the lines. Spread evenly, then bake cookie circles for 5 or 6 minutes, or until the edges are browned. Remove cookies from sheets immediately and place each cookie over an inverted glass to mold it into a tulip shape. Let cool for 5 minutes or until firm. Remove cookies from glasses and let cool completely before filling.

PLUM SAUCE

6 ripe purple plums
¼ cup water
½ cup granulated sugar
Juice of 1 lemon
1 tablespoon plum brandy

4 To make the mousse, whisk together the egg yolks, sugar, and then cornstarch. Bring the milk to a boil in a stainless-steel pot, then whisk about ¼ cup of the hot milk into the egg mixture. Return egg-milk mixture to the hot milk and bring mixture back to a light boil, stirring constantly. Cook mixture until thick again, then pour through a strainer into a bowl. Immediately add the chocolate and stir until the chocolate has melted. Let cool completely.

5 Whip the cream until it forms soft peaks, then fold the whipped cream into the chocolate mixture. Let chill for 30 minutes before using it to fill the cups.

6 Blanch the plums by first cutting an X into the bottom of each, then plunging them into boiling water for 30 seconds. Immediately put the plums into cold water, then peel, halve, and pit. Bring the water, sugar, and lemon juice to a boil. Add the plums and cook a few minutes until they are soft. Puree in a food processor, blender, or food mill, then return puree to the pot and simmer over low heat for about 5 minutes or until thickened. Skim off any foam that forms at the top. Add the brandy and cool.

7 To serve, fill each tulip cup with chocolate mousse, then spoon a little sauce over the top. Sprinkle a few pistachio nuts on top to add color and texture, and serve at once.

PURPLE PLUM SHORTCAKE

SERVES 6 TO 8

INGREDIENTS

2½ cups all-purpose flour

1 tablespoon baking powder

¼ cup + 2 tablespoons granulated sugar

Pinch of salt

½ cup (1 stick) butter, in pieces

1 large egg, lightly beaten

¼ to ½ cup buttermilk

1 pound small, ripe Italian plums, washed, halved, and pitted

1½ cups heavy cream

1 teaspoon vanilla extract

1 In a large mixing bowl, place the flour, baking powder, ¼ cup sugar, and salt. Cut in the butter until the mixture resembles coarse meal. Add the egg and the buttermilk and stir until mixture comes together and cleans the sides of the bowl. Don't add more buttermilk than necessary to get mixture to correct consistency. Wrap dough in plastic, and chill for about 30 minutes or until firm.

2 Preheat oven to 425°F. Roll dough out onto a floured surface until it measures about 10 to 12 inches in diameter and is about ¾ inch thick. Place dough circle on a baking sheet and bake shortcake for 12 minutes, or until lightly golden and crisp. Let cool.

3 Split shortcake in half horizontally and place one layer on a cake platter. Lightly crush about half the plum halves and place on top of shortcake layer. Whip the cream with the remaining sugar and the vanilla and spread across the top. Decorate whipped cream with remaining plum halves and serve, cut into wedges.

BLUEBERRY OAT CRUMBLE

SERVES 8

INGREDIENTS

1 cup (2 sticks) butter
1 cup light brown sugar
3 large eggs
1 teaspoon vanilla extract
1 cup rolled oats
1½ cups all-purpose flour
2 teaspoons baking powder
½ teaspoon salt
1 pint blueberries, washed
Whipped cream or crème
    fraîche

1 Preheat the oven to 350°F. Set out a 9-inch square baking pan.

2 In a large bowl, cream together the butter and sugar until light and fluffy. Add the eggs, one at a time, and then add the vanilla and beat well. Mix in the oats and stir.

3 Sift together the flour, baking powder, and salt. Add the dry mixture to the oat mixture and stir gently until all the flour has been incorporated. Press ⅔s of the batter into the pan and then layer with the blueberries. Pat the remaining batter over the top at random. Leave gaps between the drops of batter to let the blueberries show through.

4 Bake the dessert for 45 minutes, or until the top crust is browned and crunchy. Remove from oven and cool for 30 minutes, then serve warm with a dollop of whipped cream or crème fraîche.

HAZELNUT CHEESECAKE

SERVES 10 TO 12

INGREDIENTS

½ batch Flaky Pie Crust Dough

2 pounds cream cheese, at room temperature

½ cup heavy cream

4 large eggs

1¾ cups granulated sugar

2 teaspoons vanilla extract

1 cup ground toasted hazelnuts

¼ teaspoon salt

1 Roll out dough on a floured surface until about ⅛ inch thick, then use to line a 10-inch springform pan. Chill the dough while you prepare the filling. Preheat the oven to 325°F.

2 In a large bowl, mix the cream cheese with a wooden spoon or paddle attachment of an electric mixer until softened but not melted. Then add the cream, eggs, sugar, vanilla, hazelnuts, and salt. Mix for 2 to 3 minutes.

3 Place the springform pan on a large square of aluminum foil and lift the edges of the foil all around, wrapping the sides and bottom of the pan. This prevents leakage in or out of the water bath.

4 Pour the cream filling into the shell and place cake pan into a larger pan. Fill the pan half way with hot water and bake for 2 hours. Turn off the oven and leave the cake to cool in the oven for an additional hour. Chill, then serve. If desired, decorate with additional whole toasted hazelnuts and/or chopped nuts.

Opposite: Hazelnut Cheesecake.

LEMON CHEESECAKE WITH FRUIT SAUCE

SERVES 8

INGREDIENTS

2 cups graham cracker crumbs

1 cup (2 sticks) butter, melted

2 pounds cream cheese, at room temperature

4 large eggs

¾ cup heavy cream

1¾ cups granulated sugar

½ teaspoon salt

Juice of 3 lemons

Zest of 1 lemon

Serve this cake with a fruit sauce of your choosing, but use only fresh fruit for the best results.

1 Combine the crumbs and butter in a mixing bowl, then press mixture into the bottom and up the sides of a 9-inch springform pan. Chill until set. Preheat the oven to 325°F.

2 In the large bowl of an electric mixer, beat the cream cheese until soft and fluffy, about 5 minutes. Add the eggs, cream, sugar, and salt. Mix only until combined, then add the juice and zest and mix gently by hand only until combined.

3 Pour the cream cheese mixture into the prepared pan and place cake in a large pan filled halfway with hot water. Bake in the water bath for 2 hours, then remove cake from oven and let cool in the water bath for 1 additional hour. Chill until ready to serve.

Opposite: Fudge Brownies (page 186).

FRUIT SAUCE

2 tablespoons water
¼ cup granulated sugar
Juice of ½ lemon
*1 quart cleaned fruit, large
   pieces chopped (use
   blueberries, cherries,
   strawberries, raspberries
   or other)*

4 Prepare the sauce. Bring the water, sugar, and lemon juice to a boil and add the fruit. Stir only until the fruit is coated with the sugar mixture, then place over low heat and cook a few minutes until the fruit is soft but still whole. Pour sauce over cooled cheesecake and serve at once.

SWEETS AND TREATS

Although not pastries per se, these favorites are every bit as much fun to make and eat. They range from simple quick breads and muffins to crisp cookies, rich custards, and tempting brownies. No one would ever think of them when the words "how about some pastry?" are spoken, yet they are just too good to ignore. When the sweet cream fillings and the butter-rich doughs become too much for you, try one of these recipes for a change of pace.

HONEY HERMITS

MAKES ABOUT 1 DOZEN

INGREDIENTS

½ cup (1 stick) butter
½ cup honey
½ cup dark brown sugar
*½ teaspoon ground
 cinnamon*
*½ teaspoon ground
 allspice*
¼ teaspoon salt
2 large eggs, lightly beaten
3 tablespoons milk
2¼ cups all-purpose flour
1 teaspoon baking soda
1 cup raisins
1 cup currants
*1 cup pitted and chopped
 dates*
½ cup chopped nuts

Bar cookies like these improve with age, especially if you cut them apart and wrap them individually, then refrigerate them. These stay chewy and delicious that way.

1 Preheat the oven to 400°F. Lightly grease a large baking sheet.

2 In a large mixing bowl, cream the butter with the honey and brown sugar. Add the spices, salt, eggs, and milk and mix until smooth.

3 Sift together the flour and the baking soda, then add to the creamed mixture but do not over-mix. Fold in the fruits and nuts. Spread the mixture onto the baking sheet until about ¼ inch thick. Bake for 10 minutes, or just until set but not dried out. Let cookies cool before cutting into squares and serving.

FUDGE BROWNIES

Photo opposite page 181

MAKES 36 TO 54

INGREDIENTS

6 to 7 ounces semisweet chocolate

10 tablespoons (1 stick + 2 tablespoons) butter

4 large eggs

¼ to ½ teaspoon salt

1½ cups to 2 cups granulated sugar

2 teaspoons vanilla extract

1 cup all-purpose flour

¾ to 1 cup chopped nuts (optional)

This recipe offers you a choice. If you like a very chocolatey brownie, add the extra ounce of chocolate; if you want a sweeter brownie, add the extra ½ cup sugar; if you want a crunchy brownie, add the cup of nuts.

1 Preheat the oven to 350°F. Generously grease a 12-inch square baking pan (or use a 12 by 18-inch cookie sheet for thinner brownies).

2 Place the chocolate and butter in the top of a double boiler and melt over hot, but not boiling, water. Stir and set aside to cool.

3 Whip together the eggs, salt, sugar, and vanilla at high speed for a couple of minutes or until blended. (Note: this step will decide the texture of the brownies. Whipping the yolks and sugar helps to incorporate more air into the batter. The longer you whip, the more of a cakelike brownie you'll get, while less whipping results in a chewier and fudgier texture.) Beat until the batter starts to lighten in color and thicken just a bit, about 2 minutes.

4 Add about ¼ cup of the batter into the chocolate to temper it, then fold the chocolate mixture into the batter. Add the flour and nuts, stirring carefully so as not to deflate the batter too much. Pour the batter into the pan and bake for about 30 minutes for the 12-inch pan and 25 minutes for the baking sheet. (Note: over-baking brownies is a common problem. Time them carefully, and adjust the time if your oven is different. You'll have to experiment a little to get the correct timing for your oven.)

5 Let brownies cool in the pan for at least 30 minutes, then cut into 2-inch squares. Wrap each brownie securely in clear wrap and refrigerate to keep them tasty and fresh.

COCONUT MACAROONS

INGREDIENTS

8 ounces almond paste
½ cup granulated sugar
3 tablespoons confectioners sugar
2 large egg whites
1 cup shredded coconut
¼ teaspoon salt

1 Preheat the oven to 375°F. Lightly grease a baking sheet or line it with parchment paper.

2 In a mixing bowl, cream the almond paste with the granulated and confectioners sugars. Add the egg whites and beat well, then add the coconut and stir.

3 Fit a pastry bag with a no. 5 or 6 tip and pipe out rounds or *fleurettes* onto the baking sheet. Bake for 20 to 30 minutes, or just until golden brown.

4 Allow the macaroons to cool on the sheet for at least 15 minutes, then serve.

NOTE These can be enjoyed plain or dipped into chocolate glaze. To make a chocolate glaze, combine 2 ounces unsweetened chocolate, ½ cup heavy cream, ½ cup granulated sugar, and 1 tablespoon light corn syrup in a saucepan. Cook over low heat, stirring until the chocolate melts, then increase heat to medium and cook 5 minutes or until mixture reaches a soft ball stage on a candy thermometer (235°F.). Add ½ teaspoon vanilla and let cool slightly before dipping in macaroons.

ALMOND BUTTER COOKIES

MAKES ABOUT 2 DOZEN

INGREDIENTS

2 ounces almond paste
1 cup confectioners sugar
2 large eggs
1 cup (2 sticks) butter
1 teaspoon vanilla extract
Pinch of salt
2½ cups all-purpose flour
1 cup strawberry preserves
4 ounces semisweet
  chocolate, melted
½ cup chopped walnuts or
  almonds, toasted

1 Preheat the oven to 350°F. Lightly grease a large baking sheet or line it with parchment paper.

2 In a large mixing bowl, cream together the almond paste and the sugar. Add the eggs, one at a time, and beat until smooth and light. Add the butter, vanilla, and salt and beat again until smooth. Add the flour all at once and stir but don't over-mix, lest the cookies become tough.

3 Fill a pastry bag with a no. 5 or 6 star tip and pipe out various cookie shapes as desired, such as stars, strips, ovals, and spirals. Bake for 10 to 15 minutes, or until the cookies have set but are still very soft. If you allow the cookies to brown too much, they will be dry and prematurely stale.

4 Let cookies cool before serving. Serve plain or sandwich two together with some strawberry preserves, then dip partway in melted semisweet chocolate and coat with toasted chopped nuts.

RUGELACH

Photo opposite page 165

MAKES ABOUT 2 DOZEN

INGREDIENTS

1/4 teaspoon salt

1 cup all-purpose flour

1/2 cup (1 stick) butter, very cold

4 ounces cream cheese

1 large egg yolk mixed with 1 tablespoon milk

FILLING

1/3 cup granulated sugar

2 to 3 tablespoons ground cinnamon

1/4 cup raisins

1/2 cup chopped walnuts

1 In a large bowl, sift together the salt and flour. Cut in the cold butter and cream cheese and begin rubbing it in coarsely as you would for a pie crust. Stop rubbing the dough as soon as it holds together and still has a coarse texture. Shape into a ball, flatten slightly, and wrap in plastic wrap. Chill for at least 30 minutes.

2 Preheat the oven to 350°F. Lightly grease a large baking sheet.

3 Mix the ingredients for the filling and set aside. Turn the dough out onto a well-floured surface and start pounding the dough gently with the rolling pin to warm it slightly. Roll the dough into a rectangle that measures 8 by 14 inches. Glaze the dough with the beaten egg and sprinkle on the filling. Cut wedges from the rectangle that each measure 4 inches high and 2 inches wide.

4 Roll up each wedge and place seam side down on the baking sheet. Glaze the top of each pastry with more beaten egg and bake until golden brown, about 30 minutes.

LEMON SCONES

INGREDIENTS

2 cups all-purpose flour
1 tablespoon baking
   powder
Pinch of salt
1/3 cup granulated sugar
1/4 cup (1/2 stick) butter, in
   pieces
Zest of 2 lemons
2 large eggs, 1 separated
1/2 cup half and half

1 Preheat the oven to 450°F. In a bowl, sift together the flour, baking powder, salt, and 3 tablespoons sugar. Cut in the butter and add the zest from 1 lemon. Continue to cut in butter until mixture resembles coarse meal. Add whole egg and egg yolk, stir, and then add the half and half, blending well. Mixture should be thoroughly moistened. Stir until it becomes a soft, homogeneous dough.

2 Turn dough out onto a floured surface and knead gently for about 1 minute, then roll out until 1/2 inch thick. Cut dough into squares and then triangles and place on a baking sheet. Brush tops with beaten reserved egg white and sprinkle with remaining lemon rind and remaining sugar.

3 Bake scones for 10 to 15 minutes, or until lightly browned on top. Let cool for about 5 minutes, then serve warm, with preserves, whipped cream, or clotted Devon cream.

HAMENTASHEN

MAKES ABOUT 1 DOZEN

INGREDIENTS

2 cups all-purpose flour
3 tablespoons granulated sugar
1 teaspoon salt
⅔ cup butter, very cold
1 large egg, lightly beaten
1 cup lekvar (prune puree) or pureed apricots or another type of preserves

1 Sift together the flour, sugar, and salt. Cut in the butter until you have a coarse mixture, as you would for a flaky pie crust. However, for hamentashen it is desirable to mix this dough just a bit more, with the beaten egg, making it easier to shape. Wrap the dough in plastic and chill for at least 45 minutes.

2 Preheat the oven to 350°F. Lightly grease a baking sheet and set aside.

3 Roll the dough out on a floured surface to a thickness of about ¼ inch. Cut the dough into 3-inch squares, then cut the squares in half diagonally into triangles. Place about 1 tablespoon of filling on each triangle and lift up each corner to form a pyramid around the filling, letting some of the filling show at the top. Pinch the seams together, and brush with beaten egg.

4 Place hamentashen on the baking sheet, leaving about 2 inches between, and bake for about 20 to 25 minutes, or until golden brown. Let cool on a rack.

BANANA PECAN BREAD WITH RUM GLAZE

SERVES ABOUT 8

INGREDIENTS

1/2 cup (1 stick) butter
1 cup granulated sugar
2 large eggs
1 teaspoon vanilla extract
3 ripe bananas
2 cups all-purpose flour
1 1/2 teaspoons baking soda
2 teaspoons ground cinnamon
1/2 teaspoon salt
1 cup buttermilk
1 cup chopped pecans
4 to 6 pecan halves

GLAZE

1/2 cup dark brown sugar
1/2 cup (1 stick) butter
2 tablespoons dark rum

1 Preheat the oven to 350°F. Generously grease and flour a large loaf pan, 9 by 5 inches.

2 In a large bowl, cream together the butter and sugar until light and fluffy. Add the eggs, one at a time, and then the vanilla. Mash the bananas to a puree and then beat in with a wooden spoon. Sift together the dry ingredients, then add to the banana mixture, alternating with the buttermilk. Stir well, then add the chopped pecans.

3 Arrange the pecan halves on the bottom of the loaf pan and then pour in the batter gently so as not to move the pecans. Bake for about 1 hour, or until a tester inserted in the center comes out clean. Let cool for 10 minutes in the pan, then remove loaf from the pan and let cool completely on a rack.

4 Bring the sugar and butter for the glaze to a boil in a saucepan. Let cook over medium heat for 2 to 3 minutes until the sugar has dissolved. Stir in the rum and immediately pour hot glaze over the cooled loaf. Let glaze set for about 30 minutes at room temperature, then serve. Cut loaf.

SWEET CARNIVAL RAVIOLI

INGREDIENTS

2½ cups all-purpose flour
3 large eggs
¼ cup granulated sugar
¼ teaspoon vanilla extract
Oil for deep-frying
Confectioners sugar

FILLING

1¾ cups part-skim ricotta
½ cup granulated sugar
Pinch of ground cinnamon
Rind of ½ lemon, grated
¼ cup grated orange rind

1 Place the flour in a mound on a pastry board. Make a well in the center. Place the eggs, sugar, and vanilla in the well and stir with a fork into the flour, incorporating the flour gradually into the wet mixture. Use your hands to knead until it becomes a soft pastry dough. Chill the dough for 30 minutes.

2 Prepare the filling. Force the ricotta through a sieve. Stir the sugar, cinnamon, lemon rind, and orange rind into the ricotta and set the mixture aside.

3 On a lightly floured surface, roll half of the dough out into a thin sheet. Using half of the filling, drop tablespoons of filling about ½ inch apart on half of the sheet of dough. Fold over the other half of the dough and press the edges together to seal in the filling. Use a pastry wheel to cut the ravioli into pockets about 1½ inches square. Repeat with remaining dough.

4 Pour oil into a small saucepan to a depth of about 4 inches. When it is very hot, deep-fry the ravioli a few at a time until they are golden. Drain them on paper towels and dust with confectioners sugar before serving.

CRANBERRY SPICE BREAD

SERVES 6 TO 8

INGREDIENTS

2 cups all-purpose flour
1 teaspoon baking soda
1 teaspoon salt
1 teaspoon ground
    cinnamon
½ teaspoon ground
    allspice
¼ teaspoon grated nutmeg
1 teaspoon grated orange
    rind
1 cup halved cranberries
½ cup light raisins
½ cup walnut halves
3 tablespoons honey
3 tablespoons lemon juice
⅓ cup orange juice
½ cup + 1 tablespoon
    water
3 large eggs
¼ cup butter, melted

1 Preheat the oven to 350°F. Lightly grease a large loaf pan, 9 by 5 inches.

2 Sift together the flour, soda, salt, spices, and rind. Add the fruits and nuts and toss in the flour to coat.

3 Beat together the honey, juices, water, eggs, and melted butter. Add to the dry mixture all at once, then stir to blend well. Turn mixture into the loaf pan and bake for 50 to 60 minutes, or until a tester comes out clean.

4 Let loaf cool in the pan for 10 minutes, then remove and let cool on a rack completely before slicing. Use a serrated knife to cut slices, and serve with whipped cream.

RAISED HONEY DOUGHNUTS

MAKES ABOUT 1½ DOZEN

INGREDIENTS

2½ packages active dry
    yeast or one 1½-ounce
    cake
½ cup honey
1 tablespoon salt
2 large eggs
6 tablespoons butter,
    melted
1 tablespoon vanilla
    extract
2 cups milk, heated to
    110°F.
5 to 6 cups all-purpose
    flour
Vegetable oil for deep
    frying
Granulated sugar

Light and chewy, these doughnuts take a little more time than the deep-fried cake variety, but they are well worth it.

1 Dissolve the yeast, honey, salt, eggs, butter, and vanilla in the milk. Add the flour gradually, while kneading the mixture. Don't use all the flour unless the dough is very sticky. After kneading for 10 minutes, the dough should be smooth, elastic, and still sticking slightly to your hands. Dust lightly with flour and cover. Let rise at room temperature for about 1½ hours or until doubled in bulk.

2 Roll the dough out until about ½ inch thick, then cut out doughnut shapes. Place shapes on a greased baking sheet and let rise at room temperature for 35 to 40 minutes, or until doubled in bulk.

3 Heat the oil in a deep-frying pot until between 365° and 375°F. Drop about 4 or 5 of the doughnuts in at a time, and fry for about 20 seconds on each side, or until golden brown. Let drain on paper towels, then sprinkle with granulated sugar and serve hot.

Opposite: Raised Honey Doughnuts.

CARAMEL CUSTARD

MAKES 1 LARGE CUSTARD
SERVING 8 TO 10,
or 10 INDIVIDUAL
RAMEKINS

INGREDIENTS

4 cups milk
1 cup granulated sugar
12 large egg yolks
¼ teaspoon salt
2 teaspoons vanilla extract

CARAMEL COATING

1½ cups granulated sugar
Juice of 1 lemon, strained
Grated rind of 1 lemon

Caramel custard certainly is not a pastry, but I've included it here nonetheless. It makes an elegant presentation.

1 Select a large pan which will hold the desired baking dish or dishes. Use either a 1½-quart soufflé mold or 10 individual ¾-cup ramekins.

2 Place the milk and sugar in a saucepan and bring to a boil, whisking to dissolve all the sugar. While the milk heats, place the egg yolks, salt, and vanilla in a large bowl. When milk comes to a boil, pour ½ cup of the boiling milk mixture slowly onto the yolks to temper them, then whisk quickly to prevent lumping. Slowly pour the egg yolk mixture into the saucepan, continuing to whisk steadily. Heat gently over low heat until slightly thickened, then strain immediately through a very fine sieve into a cooled bowl. Set aside.

3 Place the sugar and lemon juice for the coating into a saucepan and cook over medium heat until it is amber colored. Add the lemon rind and stir, then pour the carmelized sugar into the bottom of the mold. Pour in just enough to cover the bottom. (Note: Be careful when handling cooked sugar; it is at an extremely high temperature and its sticky nature makes for nasty and painful burns.) Allow the caramelized molds to set and harden completely, about 30 minutes. If the caramel has not hardened sufficiently, it may dissolve into the custard above it and spoil its smooth texture.

4 Preheat the oven to 325°F. Pour the custard mixture into the mold, then place the mold into your water bath. Put bath into the oven and half fill the bath with hot water. Bake for about 1¼ hours for single custard, 40 minutes for individual custards. The bath allows the custard to bake at a more even temperature with less crusting and fewer hot spots. Also, if you are using individual molds, you'll have them all in one pan.

5 Remove custard from the oven when browned on top and no longer liquid at the center (when "set"). Separate custard from side of the mold, using a wet spoon. This is to prevent the custard from sticking to the sides of the mold when turned out onto a plate. Let cool for 5 minutes.

6 Place a plate over the mold and invert custard onto the plate. Slowly remove the mold, revealing the upside-down custard with the caramelized sugar running down the sides. Serve immediately or wrap and store to serve later.

APPLE WALNUT MUFFINS

INGREDIENTS

1½ cups all-purpose flour
½ cup light brown sugar
2 teaspoons baking powder
½ teaspoon salt
1 tablespoon ground
  cinnamon
1 cup finely chopped tart
  green apples
½ cup light raisins
½ cup chopped walnuts
½ cup sour cream
½ cup apple juice
¾ cup (1½ sticks) butter,
  melted
1 large egg
1 teaspoon vanilla extract

1 Preheat the oven to 375°F. Lightly grease a 1-dozen muffin tin. In a large bowl, sift together the flour, brown sugar, baking powder, salt, and cinnamon. Add the fruits and nuts and then toss in the flour to coat well.

2 Whisk together the sour cream, apple juice, butter, egg, and vanilla. Make a well in the center of the flour-fruit mixture and pour in the liquid ingredients. Stir with a wooden spoon until mixture is moistened. Do not over-mix; over-mixing will cause the muffins to be tough and dry. The key to tender, flaky muffins is to mix gently just to moisten the ingredients.

3 Place the muffin tin in the oven for about 5 minutes, or until hot. Remove tin from oven and quickly divide batter among the cups. Return tin to the oven and bake for about 15 minutes, or until the muffins spring back when pressed.

4 Remove muffins from oven and let cool in the cups for a few minutes, then unmold onto a rack to cool completely. Serve the muffins slightly warm or store in the freezer or refrigerator and reheat later.

DESSERT CREPES WITH APPLE-CALVADOS FILLING

MAKES ABOUT 8

INGREDIENTS

2 tablespoons butter
2 large eggs
2 tablespoons water
¼ teaspoon salt
1½ cups buttermilk
1 teaspoon grated lemon
  rind
1 cup all-purpose flour

FILLING

½ cup chopped walnuts
½ cup light raisins
¼ cup calvados
4 ripe tart apples
¼ cup (½ stick) butter
1 cup cider or apple juice
2 teaspoons lemon juice
2 teaspoons cinnamon
½ cup light brown sugar

1 Melt the butter over low heat, then let cool slightly. In a bowl, combine the melted butter, eggs, water, salt, buttermilk, and lemon rind. Gradually sift the flour into the mixture and when all the flour is completely mixed in, cover the bowl with plastic wrap and let rest for 20 minutes.

2 Lightly coat a 7-inch skillet or crepe pan with oil, using a paper towel or pastry brush. Heat the skillet or pan over medium heat and, when very hot but not smoking, pour in ¼ cup of the batter and quickly tilt the pan around to coat the bottom evenly. Cook until set, about 5 minutes. Then remove crepe from the pan by flipping it out or carefully lifting it with a pancake turner. Place on a warmed plate and continue to make remaining crepes. (Note: The crepes can be frozen. Place wax paper between them, wrap them in foil, and freeze. To reheat, wrap in foil and warm in a 375°F. oven for about 10 minutes.)

3 To prepare the filling, toast the nuts in a 350°F. oven for about 8 minutes. Combine the raisins and calvados in a small bowl and set aside. Peel, core, and halve the apples, then cut each half into 4 long slices.

4 Heat the butter in a skillet, then sauté apple slices until just soft. Bring the cider, lemon juice, cinnamon, and sugar to a boil in a saucepan, then pour into the skillet with the apples and cook until syrup begins to thicken, about 5 minutes. Stir in the nuts, raisins, and calvados.

5 Place warmed crepe on a plate and spread filling down center. Roll crepe around the filling and serve with a little sweetened whipped cream on the side.

THE FINISHING TOUCH

Often, the pastry will be all you want. If you are serving a Paris-Brest or Cream Horns, or just a Banana Cream Tart, the best presentation is the dessert itself. Perhaps, as in the case of the Cream Horns, you will just dust the horns with a bit of confectioners sugar. There are other times, however, when your dessert or pastry will call for a sauce, and you'll drizzle on some Crème Anglaise or serve it in a lovely pitcher alongside. If you have constructed an elaborate layer cake, you might prefer to decorate it with some swirls of chocolate or rosettes of whipped cream. These sauces and decorations are what is described in this chapter—the finishing touches that turn everyday cakes and pastries into elegant and fancy presents for your guests and family.

CRÈME ANGLAISE

This is a dessert sauce made without a thickener such as cornstarch or flour. Crème Anglaise (English cream) is a custard sauce and must be prepared (carefully, by tempering) like other custards such as pastry cream. Use a heavy-gauge stainless-steel or enamel pot, not aluminum because it will react and discolor your custard. Remember that this sauce must be only as thick as any savory sauce, and certainly not as thick as pastry cream. Do not let it boil or thicken over high heat.

For a basic Crème Anglaise, you'll need:

1 cup milk   *6 egg yolks*
1 cup heavy cream   *Pinch of salt*
¾ cup granulated sugar   *1 teaspoon vanilla extract*

Place the milk, cream, and sugar in a heavy-bottomed saucepan over low heat. Bring to a boil, stirring, then set aside briefly. Place the yolks, salt, and vanilla in a mixing bowl and whisk until blended. Take about ⅓ of the hot milk mixture and stir it into the yolks to temper them, then return the mixture to the saucepan, whisking steadily. Return to low heat and continue whisking, especially at the bottom where the heat is, until the sauce thickens and coats the back of a spoon. When you see wisps of steam coming from the custard, be wary—it may be getting too hot or it may almost be ready.

When the custard is just thick enough, pour it immediately through a strainer into a cool bowl. Cover with clear plastic wrap, touching the surface of the custard so that a skin won't form. Chill the custard to serve later, or serve still warm.

This is a basic recipe, and it makes about 2½ cups of custard sauce. You can vary the recipe as follows:

1. CHOCOLATE SAUCE   Add 3 to 4 ounces of chopped semisweet chocolate to the hot custard, then stir to blend well. Cover and let cool.

2. LEMON SAUCE   Omit the vanilla extract and stir in the zest of 2 lemons just before chilling.

3. FLAVORED SAUCE   Omit the vanilla extract and substitute 2 or 3 tablespoons of a flavored liqueur, such as Grand Marnier or Kahlua.

Crème Anglaise can accompany almost any dessert (on the plate, alongside the pastry; not on top). Serve it with pies or tarts, puff pastry, or my Caramelized Pear Tart.

ZABAGLIONE CREAM

This sauce is almost a sponge cake batter, without flour. Best to accompany fruit or light pastry, Zabaglione Cream is very light and very airy. This is why it must be made just before it is to be used, or it will begin to deflate. Note that there is no milk or cream in this recipe:

6 large eggs
¾ cup granulated sugar
2 tablespoons liqueur or rum
Pinch of salt

Whip the eggs, sugar, liqueur, and salt in a saucepan or bowl set over a larger pan of hot water. Set the pans over low heat and whisk until the mixture gets hot and starts to lighten and thicken, about 5 minutes. Serve immediately. (Note: Often in a restaurant, your waiter or maitre d' will prepare this at the table to ensure absolute freshness and airy consistency.) This makes 1½ cups of sauce.

FRESH FRUIT SAUCES

There is nothing so refreshing as a sauce made from puréed fresh fruits. Since fruits vary in sweetness, you'll want to add sugar to taste, but the important ingredient is the fruit itself. Use the best available, without blemishes and at its peak of ripeness. For a berry sauce, use:

2 tablespoons granulated sugar
¼ cup water
Juice of 1 lemon
*1 pint fresh berries, such as raspberries,
    strawberries, blueberries*

Cook the sugar, water, and lemon juice in a heavy-gauge pot just until the sugar is dissolved. Add the fruit and continue cooking for no more than 3 minutes—until fruit is just soft. Remove from heat and let cool. This makes 2 cups of sauce.

This sauce may be used as is or forced through a strainer to smooth it to a purée. Liqueurs may be added to enhance flavor.

When making a sauce with fresh apricots, peaches, pears, and other large fruits, first peel and pit the fruit and chop into small pieces. If desired, push the fruit through a strainer or purée in a blender or food processor before mixing with the sugary syrup in the pot. You can also add 1 or 2 tablespoons of brandy such as Kirsch or liqueur such as Grand Marnier.

NOTE: When fresh fruit is not available, you can make a fruit dessert sauce by heating 1 cup of preserves with 3 tablespoons of water or liqueur until preserves are melted, then straining the preserves if desired.

DECORATIONS

Cakes frequently look even more appetizing when they are topped with an interesting decoration. These decorations need not be elaborate, nor do they require special equipment. You can create a stunning design with some very simple steps, yet your guests will marvel at the dessert you place before them.

To make any kind of swirls, to pipe a border design, or to write a name or message on your cake, you'll need to make a paper piping cone, or coronet. Cut a triangle of parchment paper that measures about 10 inches on all 3 sides. Bring 2 corners toward the third corner so that all 3 are pointing in the same direction.

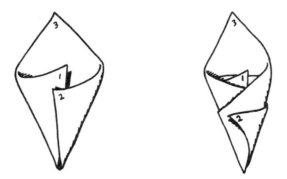

Continue to wrap the outside flap around the corners, keeping all 3 corners pointing in the same direction, until the corners meet. Then fold the corners together to keep your cone intact. Fill the cone with melted chocolate or icing until half-full, then twist the top into a knot. Cut a very small hole at the tip, so that the chocolate or icing can be piped through.

1. TOP DESIGNS   This works especially well when you pipe melted chocolate onto a white fondant coating (see Petits Fours Glacéed). Use these designs for ideas on decorating.

2. BORDER DESIGNS   Use these ideas to decorate round, square, and rectangular cakes.

You can also decorate using a pastry bag and any of a number of decorating tips. For example, you can fill the bag with flavored whipped cream. With a star tip, pipe out the filling in a circular motion, from bottom to top, to make rosettes.

Pipe a series of rosettes around the top or bottom edge of a round cake, or make a rosette in the center of the top and insert a cherry or other decoration. Never fill the pastry bag more than half-full, and when you squeeze the bag, twist the wider end, applying a steady pressure until icing or cream comes out of the nozzle evenly. In addition to rosettes, you can pipe out:

1. STRAIGHT LINES   Use a plain tip. Move along just above the line with a steady hand, using your other hand to guide the hand holding the bag. Pipe to an even thickness and stop just before the end of the line, then dip the tip down to the surface of the cake.

2. STARS   Use a star tip and hold the bag upright. Squeeze the cream out and when you have a star form, lift bag away quickly.

3. SHELLS   Use a star tip or shell tip. Hold the bag at an angle, just above surface. Squeeze until you have a form, then stop squeezing to decrease flow. Lift and then form next shell.

4. ROSES   Use a petal tip. Pipe a cone of icing in the center and then pipe several petals around the center, overlapping them. These are best made separately and then allowed to harden before placing on the cake.

There are other decorations you can use, such as:

1. CHOCOLATE CURLS   Spread melted chocolate onto a cold surface and let set just barely. Using a wide blade spatula, push at the chocolate in strips, making curls. Transfer to the cake, scattering over top. Alternatively, you can make scrapings of chocolate directly from a solid bar, using a cheese knife.

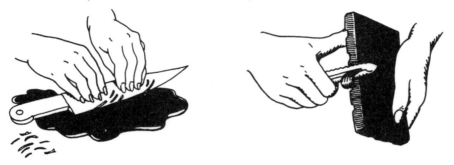

2. CANDIED VIOLETS/FROSTED GRAPES   Dip the violets or grapes into lightly beaten egg white until completely coated, then dip into a dish of superfine sugar, coating well. Shake off excess and allow to dry.

3. CHOCOLATE LEAVES Paint the back sides of firm leaves, such as ivy or roses, with an even layer of melted chocolate. Let chocolate harden in the refrigerator for about 10 minutes, then carefully peel away the leaf. The impression of the veins should remain and you'll have a chocolate leaf. Attach with a little melted chocolate to the top of your cake.

Other ways to decorate your cakes and pastries are with marzipan fruits, crushed candy, candied orange peel, and so on. If you are using a pastry dough, after baking your dessert, sprinkle the crisp baked scraps onto the sides or top. Lastly, some of the best decorations are the simplest: Sift confectioners sugar over the surface of your cake, using a pattern if desired.

GLOSSARY

The following are words generally used in the making of pastries and other desserts. I've tried to stay away from specialized terms in these recipes, but often the professional word conveys exactly what should be done in a way that is simpler and quicker to understand. You'll find some of these words used in the preceding recipes; you'll come across the remaining ones in recipes from other books.

BAKING Although this term means simply to cook something in an oven, you should bake your pastries in the center of the oven unless otherwise directed. Preheat the oven to the specified temperature before placing in your pastry. Unless indicated otherwise, avoid opening the oven door until the baking is almost completed. Test for doneness and, if necessary, continue baking until done. It is essential that your temperature settings are accurate; check them regularly with a top-quality oven thermometer, and have it recalibrated when necessary.

BEATING   Oftentimes, the term *beat* is used synonymously with *mix,* meaning that you combine ingredients until smooth and evenly blended. This is best done with a wooden spoon or electric mixer. When egg whites or heavy cream are beaten, you are incorporating air into the eggs or cream. This is best done with a wire whisk or electric mixer.

CREAM   To cream together butter and sugar, smear them with the back of a spoon or use an electric mixer to mix until they form a smooth, light paste. Alternately, you could cream them together with your hand but you risk warming the butter too much. Well-creamed butter will be smooth and light, not greasy.

CUT IN   When you cut butter into flour, you break up the butter into small particles and coat them with flour until you have a homogeneous mixture that resembles coarse meal. You can cut in with a fork or two butter knives, or use your hands to break apart the butter.

FOLD   When you've beaten egg whites or cream and want to incorporate them into your mixture, you will stir them in gently so as to avoid deflating them. This is called *folding.* Fold in with a rubber spatula or use your hands, keeping your fingers spread apart. Reach down into the bottom and bring your hand up through, repeating only until the mixtures are combined.

KNEAD   Heavy doughs, such as those for yeast-risen pastries, are kneaded until they are smooth and elastic. To knead, turn out the dough onto a lightly floured surface and fold the dough in half, then push against it with the heel of your hand. Turn and press, then sprinkle lightly with flour if the dough is sticky. Knead for the specified time, or until dough springs back lightly.

ROLL OUT   Especially when making a pie crust, you will mix your dough, then roll it out on a flat surface until it is the thickness or size specified in the recipe. Use a good rolling pin and dust the surface of your counter to prevent the dough from sticking to it. Roll out, pressing evenly with the rolling pin, to have a crust with an equal thickness throughout; avoid pressing harder at the ends of the dough, either as you begin to roll or as you finish because that will destroy the texture of the pastry.

SIFT   Dry ingredients, such as flour or baking powder, should be sifted, or shook through a strainer or sifter to remove lumps and break up large clumps. All-purpose flour is sold most often as presifted nowadays, but it is still advisable to sift your dry ingredients together before using. This sifting will lighten the dry items and more thoroughly blend them. All quantities in this book are for presifted flour.

SOURCES

Just about all the equipment and ingredients used in the preceding recipes are readily available, either in supermarkets or in gourmet kitchenware shops. However, if you can't find what you want, the following are additional sources which deal in mail order.

INGREDIENTS

Balducci's, 424 Avenue of the Americas, New York, New York 10011 (212) 673-2600.

Dean & DeLuca, 121 Prince Street, New York, New York 10012 (212) 254-7774.

H. Roth & Son, 1577 First Avenue, New York, New York 10028 (212) 734-1110

Maid of Scandinavia, 3244 Raleigh Avenue, Minneapolis, Minnesota 55416 (800) 328-6722.

Williams-Sonoma, 576 Sutter Street, San Francisco, California 94119 (415) 652-1515.

EQUIPMENT

Bridge Kitchenware Corp., 214 East 52 Street, New York, New York 10022 (212) 688-4220.

Chef's Catalog, 3915 Commercial Avenue, Northbrook, Illinois 60062 (312) 480-9400.

Kitchen Bazaar, 4455 Connecticut Avenue N.W., Washington, D.C. 20008 (212) 363-4625.

Nussex Bakery Equipment Company, 14752 Franklin Avenue, Tustin, California 92680 (714) 832-9956.

Williams-Sonoma, 576 Sutter Street, San Francisco, California 94119 (415) 652-1515.

BAKING MEASUREMENTS

Here are some general kitchen measurements which may be of help in your baking. These measurements are for U.S. cooks.

3 teaspoons = 1 tablespoon
4 tablespoons = ¼ cup
5⅓ tablespoons = ⅓ cup
8 tablespoons = ½ cup

1 cup = ½ pint or 8 fluid ounces
2 cups = 1 pint or 16 fluid ounces
1 quart (liquid) = 2 pints or 4 cups
1 gallon (liquid) = 4 quarts

5 whole eggs = 1 cup
8 to 10 egg whites = 1 cup
10 to 12 egg yolks = 1 cup

8 tablespoons butter = ½ cup or 1 stick
2 sticks butter = 1 cup
2 cups butter = 1 pound

3 packages active dry yeast = 1 cake yeast
1 package active dry yeast = 1 scant tablespoon

1 square chocolate = 1 ounce or 1 tablespoon melted
1 ounce unsweetened chocolate = ⅓ cup cocoa powder

1 pound apples = 3 cups peeled, cored, and sliced
6 ounces raisins = 1 cup
¼ pound walnuts will yield 1 cup shelled
1 pound walnuts will yield ½ pound shelled

1 lemon yields 2½ to 3½ tablespoons juice
1 orange yields 5 to 6 tablespoons juice

12 ounces honey = 1 cup
1 pound confectioners sugar = 3½ cups
1 pound brown sugar = 2¼ cups
1 pound granulated sugar = 2 cups

1 pound flour = approximately 4 cups
1 pound cake flour = 4½ cups
1 pound whole wheat flour = 3¾ cups

CONVERSION TABLES

The following are conversion tables and other information applicable to those converting the recipes in this book for use in other English-speaking countries. The cup and spoon measures given in this book are U.S. Customary (cup = 236 mL; 1 tablespoon = 15 mL). Use these tables when working with British Imperial or Metric kitchen utensils.

LIQUID MEASURES

The Imperial pint is larger than the U.S. pint; therefore note the following when measuring the liquid ingredients.

U.S.	IMPERIAL
1 cup = 8 fluid ounces	1 cup = 10 fluid ounces
½ cup = 4 fluid ounces	½ cup = 5 fluid ounces
1 tablespoon = ¾ fluid ounce	1 tablespoon = 1 fluid ounce

U.S. MEASURE	METRIC*	IMPERIAL*
1 quart (4 cups)	950 mL	1½ pints + 4 tablespoons
1 pint (2 cups)	450 mL	¾ pint
1 cup	236 mL	¼ pint + 6 tablespoons
1 tablespoon	15 mL	1 + tablespoon
1 teaspoon	5 mL	1 teaspoon

*Note that exact quantities are not always given. Differences are more crucial when dealing with larger quantities. For teaspoon and tablespoon measures, simply use scant or generous quantities; or for more accurate conversions, rely upon metric.

Solid Measures

Outside the U.S., cooks measure more items by weight. Here are approximate equivalents for basic items in this book.*

	U.S. CUSTOMARY	METRIC	IMPERIAL
Apples (peeled and chopped)	2 cups	225 g	8 ounces
Butter	1 cup	225 g	8 ounces
	½ cup	115 g	4 ounces
	¼ cup	60 g	2 ounces
	1 tablespoon	15 g	½ ounce
Chocolate chips	½ cup	85 g	3 ounces

	U.S. CUSTOMARY	METRIC	IMPERIAL
Coconut (shredded)	½ cup	60 g	2 ounces
Fruit (chopped)	1 cup	225 g	8 ounces
Nut Meats (chopped)	1 cup	115 g	4 ounces
Raisins (and other dried fruits)	1 cup	175 g	6 ounces
Sugar (granulated)	1 cup	190 g	6½ ounces
	½ cup	85 g	3 ounces
or caster	¼ cup	40 g	1¾ ounces
(confect-	1 cup	80 g	2⅔ ounces
tioners) or	½ cup	40 g	1⅓ ounces
icing	¼ cup	20 g	¾ ounces

*So as to avoid awkward measurements, some conversions are not exact.

INDEX